ASPATORE
BOOKS

INSIDE THE MINDS:
The Financial Services Industry

The Future of Financial Services –
Risks, Opportunities & Areas to Watch

Published by Aspatore Books, Inc.
For corrections, company/title updates, comments or any other inquiries please email info@aspatore.com.

First Printing, 2002
10 9 8 7 6 5 4 3 2 1

ISBN 1-58762-062-6

Library of Congress Card Number: 2002091998

Cover design by Kara Yates & Ian Mazie

Edited by Jo Alice Hughes, Proofread by Ginger Conlon

Material in this book is for educational purposes only. This book is sold with the understanding that neither any of the authors or the publisher is engaged in rendering legal, accounting, investment, or any other professional service.

This book is printed on acid free paper.

A special thanks to all the individuals that made this book possible.

Special thanks to: Kirsten Catanzano, Melissa Conradi, Molly Logan, Justin Hallberg

The views expressed by the individuals in this book do not necessarily reflect the views shared by the companies they are employed by (or the companies mentioned in this book). The companies referenced may not be the same company that the individual works for since the publishing of this book.

The views expressed by the endorsements on the cover of this book for the *Inside the Minds* series do not necessarily reflect the views shared by the companies they are employed by. The companies referenced may not be the same company that the individual works for since the publishing of this book.

www.Aspatore.com

Aspatore Books is the largest and most exclusive publisher of C-Level executives (CEO, CFO, CTO, CMO, Partner) from the world's most respected companies. Aspatore annually publishes a select group of C-Level executives from the Global 1,000, top 250 professional services firms, law firms (Partners & Chairs), and other leading companies of all sizes. C-Level Business Intelligence™, as conceptualized and developed by Aspatore Books, provides professionals of all levels with proven business intelligence from industry insiders – direct and unfiltered insight from those who know it best – as opposed to third-party accounts offered by unknown authors and analysts. Aspatore Books is committed to publishing a highly innovative line of business books, and redefining such resources as indispensable tools for all professionals. In addition to individual best-selling business titles, Aspatore Books publishes the following lines of unique books, reports and journals: Inside the Minds, Executive Reports, and C-Level Quarterly Journals. Aspatore is a privately held company headquartered in Boston, Massachusetts, with employees around the world.

Inside the Minds

The critically acclaimed *Inside the Minds* series provides readers of all levels with proven business intelligence from C-Level executives (CEO, CFO, CTO, CMO, Partner) from the world's most respected companies. Each chapter is comparable to a white paper or essay and is a future-oriented look at where an industry/profession/topic is heading and the most important issues for future success. Each author has been carefully chosen through an exhaustive selection process by the *Inside the Minds* editorial board to write a chapter for this book. *Inside the Minds* was conceived in order to give readers actual insights into the leading minds of business executives worldwide. Because so few books or other publications are actually written by executives in industry, *Inside the Minds* presents an unprecedented look at various industries and professions never before available.

INSIDE THE MINDS:
The Financial Services Industry
The Future of Financial Services –
Risks, Opportunities & Areas to Watch

CONTENTS

Angelo R. Mozilo   9
LEADERSHIP AND THE FUTURE OF
THE FINANCIAL SERVICES INDUSTRY

Scott A. McAfee   33
A LEADER'S PERSPECTIVE: WHAT IT
WILL TAKE TO REMAIN A LEADER IN
FINANCIAL SERVICES

Edward G. McLaughlin   67
THE CREATIVE MANAGEMENT OF
STRATEGIC RELATIONSHIPS FOR
LONG-TERM SUCCESS

Michael P. Duffy   83
BRINGING THE WORLD TOGETHER
THROUGH COMMERCE

James L. (Jim) Hunter   103
OVER THE FENCE: A PEEK INSIDE A
TOP-TIER CANADIAN FIRM

Ralph H. Clinard   **119**
NICHE MARKETING AND THE
IMPORTANCE OF BEING OPPORTUNISTIC

James C. Smith   **135**
FINDING A WAY

LEADERSHIP AND THE FUTURE OF THE FINANCIAL SERVICES INDUSTRY

ANGELO R. MOZILO
Countrywide Credit Industries, Inc.

Chairman, President, and
Chief Executive Officer

Visions of Tomorrow's Industry

Leading a financial services company. There's no end to the resources for advice about and techniques for leadership. And opinions about the future of financial services are equally plentiful.

Generally, for a financial services company, or any company for that matter, success boils down to leadership that has a vision for the future, plans how to get there, and ensures the plans are executed. Sounds simple, right? Well, of course, it is and it isn't. These are three separate abilities and skill sets. Think about it.

A leader must be a visionary, able to literally visualize where the company will go in the future. Planning and strategizing then come into play as you build a company to prosper, grow, and last. Then, it takes true interpersonal skills to lead employees to implement and execute the plan. It is the rare leader who can do all three. Most CEOs excel at one or two.

The success of Countrywide speaks for itself. I cannot define what model will be successful for everyone. I can only share the experiences I have had with Countrywide. But, since the best piece of advice I have ever been given is, "Never give up on a dream or in something or someone of significance to you," I encourage you to read on.

Today, and for the foreseeable future, the two major drivers of financial services are industry consolidation and technology. To succeed with consumers who will demand an increasingly wider variety of personal finance products and services at the lowest possible cost, you will have to be of significant size. You will have to have scale. You will have to have capital. And you will have to make enormous investments in technology.

Growth Through Consolidation

For at least the past five to seven years, the trend toward consolidation, primarily through mergers and acquisitions, has been the biggest news in financial services. The trend was given a big boost with the enactment of Gramm-Leach-Bliley, enabling companies of all sizes to enter diverse financial services for the first time since the Glass-Steagall Act was signed in 1933. We may think the consolidation during the 1990s was profound, but it was nothing compared to what we'll see in the future in financial services.

Again, success will require scale, capital, and investment. Companies that can't meet the requirements – and there will be many – will become candidates for consolidation. We will all face challenges as competitors become larger and structure themselves for competitive advantage by highly leveraging capital.

Historically, mortgage banking companies had been relatively small mom-and-pop-type operations and some midsize operations. Countrywide vaulted to the number one position in the early and mid-1990s by focusing on technology and new ways of doing business. However, over the past three or four years, huge companies acquired an amazing number of mortgage companies and became major competitors. So how did Countrywide prosper? When consolidation takes place, there can be tremendous disruption for both the acquired and the acquiring companies. That disruption creates opportunity for us. Countrywide can attract top-performing personnel, who may have become disoriented, displaced, or disillusioned. And, since consolidation can have an impact on customers who become frustrated with the chaotic changes inherent in offices closing and people leaving, we aggressively pursue those customers and increase our market share.

As the Countrywide example illustrates, CEOs and other leaders must face and solve cultural issues during consolidation – not an easy task. As I touched on before, merging the cultures of two distinct organizations also means merging the ever-changing attitudes of employees who work for you. And how do you do that effectively?

I am old enough to remember when the way to run a company effectively was to be a dictator. Then, if you were really advanced, you were a benevolent dictator. Now, management is participatory – your people participate in the strategic process. So merging attitudes requires leaders to seek out new ways of communicating the company's core values, mission, and vision.

Consolidation in the future will also require CEOs to manage increasingly complex execution. When you are a single business, processing and originating mortgages for example, that is complex enough. But when you are dealing with other financial products, and you are global in nature, as a CEO you need to surround yourself with a team that can deal with all of these businesses effectively. You need to upgrade the management team that surrounds you. Everything flows from that. It is important to get people in those positions who are best in class and understand the mission. Consolidation will further enhance the importance of a solid organizational structure and having the right people in the right positions.

Taking Technology to the Top

Technology will continue to play a major role in the financial services industry. More and more people will want round-the-clock access to their finances, particularly young people who have grown up using computers and the Internet. Customers will demand a point-and-click environment for financial services. We are already seeing it happen, and growth is almost exponential.

How will successful leaders respond? By staying one step ahead of technology and understanding what future technological developments will happen. Investments in technology can be incredibly costly, and the technology itself changes so rapidly, that you have to stay current – not just on what's happening today, but also what's in development. You need to have some idea of what technology will look like five and even 10 years down the road. How does a CEO do this?

First, you must maintain a close relationship with the company's chief technology officer, as well as with other members of your

IT team. These individuals have both the expertise and the experience. They can be great educators. But you also want to ensure that the technology vision matches business realities. That's why CEOs should try to attend technology conferences and learn on their own, as well. I have found these events can be absolutely revelatory. Any time there is anything involved with technology related to my business, I try to take advantage of it. A lot of technocrats have booths at financial services conventions, so I go there to see what's happening. I try to stay abreast of the latest technological efforts under way. From time to time I go to the laboratories of IBM and try to get a glimpse of what they see and what they are doing for the future. IBM has equipment and computers they will release three or four years from now that are already built. Another example is Microsoft. They have conferences from time to time, and when they invite me, I am always there.

Technology conferences are also important because you get to look beyond your industry. One of the best ideas I saw had to do with trucking – tracking where trucks are and where the commodities in those trucks are going. Today Countrywide Home Loans uses a similar system to track loan status.

As for future technologies, there are several that I believe may have a significant impact on the financial services industry. They are being driven by the demands of consumers and investors. Consumers are increasingly expressing a preference for doing business with primarily one or two vendors. They do not want their personal finances spread out all over the industry. It's too cumbersome and too time-consuming, robbing them of leisure time and other things important in their personal lives. To be a successful financial services company, you have to be comprehensive and easy to use. Consumers prefer to deal with one or two companies that provide them with state-of-the-art technology and low-cost products and services.

With financial services providers offering everything from insurance to checking accounts, the key to meeting these needs will be technology that supports integration – systems and applications that allow customers to have online access to all products and services with virtually one click. The goal is to have consumers be able to migrate from one Internet page to another, or one company's site to another's, using a single password and a single click. Whether they are buying insurance, getting a mortgage, or ordering an appraisal, they are able to navigate the Web seamlessly. Everything is and will be driven by technology that provides not only a point-and-click environment but, more important, an information-gathering place, an encyclopedia of information.

I also believe various CRM (customer relationship management) technologies will maintain their vital role in company infrastructure. We must make large efforts to gain a better understanding of the personal preferences and needs of individual customers and how we can better serve each individual. We take customer service very seriously. In fact, Countrywide was recently ranked number one in customer satisfaction among the largest national home mortgage lenders by J.D. Power and Associates. We are committed to remaining at the top of our industry in the delivery of first-class customer service. To help achieve this Countrywide is working very closely with Siebel Systems on CRM technology. This is a departure for us. Traditionally Countrywide has successfully developed its own technology. But we conducted extensive research and recognized our need for a system to enhance our current technology.

Planning for the Future

Whether you are building a house or building a company to last 100 years, you must think about both internal and external issues – and successfully join the two.

When creating plans for the future of a company, the first thing to do is define the business by identifying the business you want to be in. This may sound overly simplistic. It's not. It is the key to success, because the definition of your business changes continuously, and it represents the message that must be understood by all who are involved with the company.

I continuously redefine Countrywide's business. If you asked me 10 years ago what I wanted our company to be, I would have said I wanted it to be the best mortgage banking company in the world. I would give you a very different answer now. I want Countrywide to be a diversified financial services powerhouse that has counter-cyclical operations, so that we are not susceptible to ever-changing interest rates and economic environments. By launching subsidiaries, like Countrywide Bank, a division of Treasury Bank, N.A., and Balboa Life & Casualty, which are not directly affected by interest rate volatility, we have already seen more steady and level financials.

The next step is to figure out what the strategic mission going forward must be to meet that definition. It is what I look at on an ongoing basis to make sure we deal with change appropriately. We've seen such great companies as Polaroid, Kodak, and Xerox – which appeared to be impenetrable, tremendously powerful companies, both financially and in brand – fall to states where they are or have been on the brink of bankruptcy. Why? I think the environment kept changing and they did not.

When planning internal matters, I'm always looking for and toward change. But very few people like change. Change is extremely important; change involves risk. So it becomes important to remind employees that it is better to be an agent of change than its victim. You underscore the importance of change by reminding them where you are headed and why you are headed there.

Successful planning must also take external factors into consideration. For consumer-based financial services firms, that means focusing on the customer. All plans must be customer-centric. If it's not good for the customer, it is not good for the company. The CEO has the major task of ensuring that bureaucracy does not dominate and that we do not just do things that are good for the company, irrespective of their impact on the customer. It is critical to have someone in the organization with enormous power to be an advocate for the customer.

Before I started Countrywide I was the guy in the field you went to if you needed to borrow money to buy a home. I processed loans, collected the payments, called the delinquents, and shipped the loan. I did everything. As a result I gained an intimate knowledge of what the customer wanted. At Countrywide today I am still translating those needs and incorporating them into our products and services. I want to ensure that we are listening to customers and delivering products and services that meet their needs, not ours.

For example, an average customer's mortgage loan file today contains 70 to 80 pieces of paper. That number should be one, maybe two, period. And it should be scanned into a database at the end of the process, and the paper reused or recycled. There would be no need for vaults or billions of file folders. The closing process should be simplified substantially in size and scope, and the underwriting of loans should be made much easier. We should do paperless underwriting, depending mostly upon technology to do the process. What does that mean? It means maybe there are no appraisals, maybe there is no title insurance policy anymore, and maybe there are no security instruments anymore. All of this work can be done electronically. All of this would be very, very good for the consumer and for businesses. A lot of groups would scream and yell about that – not because it is not good for the consumer, but because it is not good for them. I believe everybody would be better served, including title companies and attorneys, if we could make this a virtually paperless, point-and-click entry process for the consumer. The bottom line is that by simplifying the process, we lower the cost and thereby create the opportunity for greater homeownership.

If you stay customer-centric, a company's needs are taken care of automatically. Once you start developing products and services with the sole purpose of making the company more comfortable, you venture down a very dangerous track. You must focus on customers.

Finally, planning requires taking risks. I believe that to succeed and grow, whether in your personal life or in business, you have to take risks. You will never improve your skiing if you never try the higher hills. You do not know what the results will be until you try to measure that risk. In my opinion, executives cannot say they are going to take a risk, while at the same time refuse to accept failure. Rarely can a person calculate the downside if he or she is engaged in a meaningful venture.

I have been the proponent of a lot of risk-taking at Countrywide. Some risks have been very good, and some of them have been horrible – more horrible than I anticipated. I learned that taking the right kind of risk involves encouraging people to think differently, to constantly be looking for other ways to generate revenues and understand that there will be risk involved. All I ask is that they make certain everybody understands the risk and that the colleagues agree on whatever venture they are going to enter, including my endorsement. We then go out and try to execute the best we can.

Execution: Your True Test as a Leader

For a company to execute properly, everyone in that organization has to be in concert with one another. It starts with an understanding of two things: Execution is extraordinarily important, and no one in the organization can tolerate mediocrity in the execution process.

I personally sit down and review each major area of the company on an ongoing basis to see how we are executing. I inquire about several things. What has happened to volumes or revenues? What has happened to expenses? What has happened to net income? How are consumers reacting to our products? What feedback are we getting? I look at a wide variety of other things, which most people define as review of execution. A CEO should spend most of his or her time on this activity in various ways, both internally and externally.

Internally, a review of execution involves going to your facilities on a continuous basis and talking to people personally about their views of their jobs and of the company. This way, I have direct communication with the employees involved. Externally, I have open lines – telephone and e-mail – that encourage customers to contact me. And they do, every day, telling me about the good things we do and the bad things we do. I have direct communication with those affected by the execution. In terms of the quality of information I get, I find the complaints from customers to be important and educational. They ensure we continue to improve execution.

Regardless of who you interact with, interpersonal skills will make or break a leader. You can have all of the vision and planning skills in the world, but without quality communication with those who do the heavy lifting, the degree of success will shrink.

Characteristics of a Successful Leader

To become a leader you need first and foremost to have a strong desire to lead, which is often innate. It is a strong desire to be number one in a group. But it is not all about some mysterious charisma that one person is just born with. You can observe and learn. Look for common traits among those you admire; then develop those skills

I am an avid observer of others. I observe successful people. I once asked Chi Chi Rodriquez how you develop a swing. He said to watch guys with great swings. I try to watch guys like Jack Welch and Warren Buffet. I notice people who I think are great leaders and try to discern what they have that makes them great. If I don't have those qualities, I try to model them. Over time, as I keep modeling those qualities, I see progress. Remember, most people do not wake up with great leadership qualities. Something has to drive the individual toward them. I had to drive myself to be a leader, and I had to strive to be number one. I always believed, as foolish as it may sound, that I could do it and do it better.

You must have the ability to inspire other people to follow you. Often, the best way to inspire and motivate is to lead by example. I always have. I want to be the first one in to work and the last one out. I want to demonstrate a work ethic that is hard to meet and exceed, because it stimulates my employees to work hard. I want them to see that it can be done and, more important, that I am willing to get into the trenches with them. I think one of the strongest aspects of my leadership is that people know I have been there. I am not a caretaker. I am not somebody who has been brought in from the outside with no knowledge of the business. The employees have a sense of appreciation for that and therefore a degree of respect, which makes it easier for me in my communication with them.

Keep employees excited about what they're doing. Give them a sense of satisfaction in what they are attempting to accomplish each day, and keep them apprised of the result of their efforts. This is especially important for large financial service companies where a particular individual's day-to-day responsibilities might not be directly linked with the result.

Integrity is an essential element of leadership. In fact, one of the most important golden rules of the financial services industry is integrity. If you want to be around for a hundred years, everyone in the organization at all levels must be focused on integrity, honesty, and clarity.

A leader must be responsive – immediately – today, not tomorrow. If somebody calls, you return the call, no matter who called or where you are. When I call Warren Buffet, he will call me back that same day, wherever he is in the world. Everybody has to be equal in terms of priority, whether it is a board member, a fellow employee, a customer, a shareholder, or a business partner.

Stay personally and intimately in touch with all aspects of the operation. People must know you are involved. I leave my office and just walk the floors. People see me and know I am concerned about them and about the company. This does not mean you control everything; it means you're providing guidance while giving people a lot of room to do what they believe is in the best interest of the company. After all, we really do learn most from our mistakes. I am not prepared for employees to repeat mistakes, but they can make mistakes.

You must have adequate communications skills. This does not mean you have to be a knockout speaker, but you have to have the means to deliver a message that people will understand, a message that encourages them to move in new or different directions. Additionally, you have to make the future come alive in people's minds, and the vision should be as clear as your own.

Never tolerate mediocrity, and always surround yourself with people who are smarter than you are. That is the greatest job security in the world. I believe the failure of many business executives today is their insecurity. They believe they will lose their jobs if they hire people smarter than they are. They settle for mediocre employees who do a mediocre job, which results in a mediocre company. A company cannot rise above the quality of its people; it is impossible. Moreover, smart people hire smart people. Stupid people hire stupid people. It's that simple. Countrywide was built on this premise. We had an idea and made that idea come to life, and once in a while the idea would be successful and stimulate someone to say, "This guy is not nuts. Let's work with him."

Continuously measure and evaluate success. Every day you must ask questions like these: How do the employees feel about what they are doing and what they are accomplishing? How do the investors feel about the value we have added or not added to their investment? How does the board feel about my performance and the overall performance of the company? How does the customer feel about the company?

All of these characteristics are combined with high energy levels and a very strong work ethic. A leader must not tolerate mediocrity and must be surrounded by the best. These are the key elements in becoming a sustainable leader who leads for the long term – for example, Hank Greenberg, who has led AIG for 40 years. He is an extraordinary leader. Another leader I believe is extremely inspiring is former GE CEO, Jack Welch. I consider him an extraordinarily impressive visionary who understands what it takes to lead and grow.

As I mentioned earlier, the best piece of business advice I ever received was to "Never give up." If you are an entrepreneur, you run into a lot of obstacles. When you do run into them, it often feels like a machine gun coming at you with no relief in sight. It is very easy to say, "I give up. I just can't do this anymore – too many sleepless nights." Or, "I'm working hard, yet going no place, and everybody is against me."

There is a great value in not giving up. If you believe in what you are doing, believe you are best of class in terms of the organization, not necessarily as an individual but as an organization, then you should not give up. When David Loeb and I cofounded Countrywide, things were rough. I had absolutely no money; we were negative on our balance sheet. He said, "Angelo, don't give up." And I didn't.

Today, Countrywide is a diversified financial services provider conducting business around the globe. In large part, I believe it is because we never gave up.

The company was built on three basic principles. They were the hallmark of the company in 1968 and they still are today: Lower the cost of financing homes; lower the barriers to entry for homeowners; and educate the consumer about mortgage banking. That is the soul of our company, and what everybody understands and can articulate and focus on. This gives us a sustainable and immutable purpose. Through our financial services, we can make a very positive difference in people's lives. Homeownership is fundamental in this country. It is fundamental to the people, and it is a very basic part of human nature to want many of the things Countrywide can help provide.

We are facilitating something that is basic to the makeup of people's dreams and goals, as well as a strong economy.

We have diversified our business over the years. Today we successfully operate insurance, capital markets, global mortgages, technology, and consulting business units. Early in 2002 we launched Countrywide Bank, a division of Treasury Bank, N.A. We're providers of financial services to consumers and businesses. Yet some things have remained the same. We never give up. And we have a sustainable purpose.

Angelo R. Mozilo, who cofounded Countrywide Credit Industries, Inc. in 1969, is chairman, president, and chief executive officer. He also serves as chairman of Countrywide Home Loans, Inc., the company's main subsidiary.

Countrywide, a global leader in residential finance and related services and a member of the S&P 500 and Forbes 500, maintains more than 500 offices across the country, with a work force of more than 21,000 employees. A hands-on manager, Mr. Mozilo is active in all aspects of Countrywide's businesses. While he reviews all financial and operational activities, his central focus is on overall business growth and strategic direction.

Mr. Mozilo was the 1991-1992 president of the Mortgage Bankers Association of America (MBA), which represents more than 3,000 member firms involved in every aspect of mortgage and real estate finance. Inducted into the National Association of Home Builders (NAHB) Hall of Fame in 1995, Mr. Mozilo currently serves on the National Housing Endowment Foundation, the philanthropic arm of the NAHB.

Other activities include serving on the boards of the National Italian American Foundation and the Harvard Kennedy School for Housing Studies. He is also a member of the Board of Trustees at Fordham University in New York City and Gonzaga University in Spokane, Washington. Mr. Mozilo served as president of the San Gabriel Valley Council of the Boy Scouts in 1993 and 1994.

Awards received by Mr. Mozilo include the Ellis Island Medal of Honor, which is held by all living U.S. Presidents; the Albert Schweitzer Award for his work with the youth of America; the Special Achievement Award for Humanitarian Service from the National Italian American Foundation; the 1999 Executive of the

Year award, presented at the MBA Western Secondary Market Conference; and the Jane Wyman Humanitarian Service Award from the Arthritis Foundation.

Mr. Mozilo received a bachelor of science degree from Fordham University in 1960 and holds an honorary doctor of laws degree from Pepperdine University.

A LEADER'S PERSPECTIVE: WHAT IT WILL TAKE TO REMAIN A LEADER IN FINANCIAL SERVICES

SCOTT A. MCAFEE

WMC Mortgage Corporation

President and Chief Executive Officer

Owning the American Dream

"We'd jus' live there. We'd belong there. There wouldn't be no more runnin' round the country. ... No, sir, we'd have our own place where we belonged and not sleep in no bunk house."

– John Steinbeck, *Of Mice and Men*

"The moral power of the nation rests on the home, the schoolhouse, and the place of worship. The government looks after education and few churches are overcrowded. But home owners are too few."

– President Calvin Coolidge

"The 4th Amendment and the personal rights it secures have a long history. At the very core stands the right of a man to retreat into his own home and there be free from unreasonable governmental intrusion."

– Potter Stewart, Associate Justice, U.S. Supreme Court

Homeownership is an essential part of the American ethos. The mechanisms to acquire a home – financial and banking institutions, markets, government entities, public policy, tax laws, technology advances – all work in concert, making home ownership an affordable reality for people with modest incomes and impaired credit. More Americans own homes today than at any other time in history. Since I entered the mortgage industry, home ownership has risen from 40 percent of all households to nearly 70 percent.

There are certain obstacles. The purchase of a home for most people is the largest and scariest financial transaction of one's life. Because of the financial risks involved, protections and regulations to both borrower and lender have created a system that is a nightmare of documents. These mechanisms exist in a constant state of flux.

The challenge of the mortgage industry is to expand homeownership opportunities by creating products, services, and technologies that help more people own homes by making the process more convenient and efficient, while reducing costs to produce and thereby making profits for the industry. The Internet and e-commerce offer great promise in this regard. The mortgage industry in the near future is facing consolidation: Many companies will exit or be subsumed into larger companies. Successful companies will be the ones whose leaders possess the vision to accommodate the constant regulatory change, leverage e-business technology solutions, reduce operating costs, and harness the human capital to make the American Dream come true for families, communities, and the nation.

Who We Are, What We Do

As a young public accountant, I remember a meeting in the office of a divisional CFO at General Mills. On his desk was a box of cereal. "This is what we make," he said. In manufacturing you are dealing with a tangible product that can be seen, inspected, touched, and improved. Our situation is entirely different: We deal in money – an abstract, symbolic exchange medium.

The absence of a tangible product requires that people in our industry have the aptitude and skill to handle and analyze financial data and information. From the intellectual capital standpoint, the financial services industry is unavoidably challenging. There is a rather steep learning curve to get an employee to the point where he or she can actually understand how to close loans in 50 different states, each with varying documentation and different laws.

The typical financial service product is so complex and supported by such a preponderance of legal documentation; it is an entirely daunting endeavor for the average consumer. It takes about 200 documents in a loan file to consummate the average home purchase in most states. To complete the loan process, a variety of specialized supporting players and participants are involved to supply the necessary products and services related to the purchase of a home and the transfer of ownership from seller to buyer. These include lenders, mortgage brokers, mortgage servicers, insurers, appraisers, title insurers, and government-sponsored enterprises (or GSEs, also known as Fannie Mae and Freddie Mac more about them later). Documents are needed for the purchase contract, realtor contracts and indemnification, property disclosures, pest control, site inspection, roof inspection, geological survey, property associations, title insurance, mortgage insurance, and the most complex product, the mortgage itself. The mortgage industry, in an attempt to meet the demands of a variety of consumers' needs, has created and offers literally hundreds of different lending products.

Since the average person is untrained and unfamiliar with the process and products, the mortgage broker has flourished in simplifying the process and in guiding the consumer through it. Mortgage brokers are intermediaries who assist borrowers with the process of selecting, finding, and securing a loan from a multitude of lenders. They choreograph the sophisticated ballet of all the related businesses whose input is required to help potential homeowners finance the home of their dreams.

In wholesale loan origination, our company's sector of the industry, our customers are the mortgage brokers. By recent estimates, 30,000 mortgage brokerage companies employ about 240,000 people, according to the industry's trade association, the National Association of Mortgage Brokers (NAMB). Mortgage brokers account for more than half of all home loans. We deal exclusively with these intermediaries, rather than directly with the borrower, as in retail lending.

Wholesale Lending: Three Sales, Three Customers

One of the unique aspects of our industry is that our products are sold three different times to three different customers. We must first create a mortgage product attractive to the actual consumer – attractive in the sense that it is competitive with that of other lenders, and that it fits the borrower's current and potential earnings.

The predominant type residential lending options are fixed-rate and adjustable-rate mortgages. Fixed-rate mortgages have an unchanging payment throughout the life of the loan – usually 15 or 30 years. Adjustable-rate mortgages, by comparison, are tied to interest rate increases or decreases. Other products that have been developed to meet the specific needs of borrowers include balloon mortgages, graduated payment, and reverse mortgages. Mortgage lenders make their lending decisions by looking at some basic factors: a person's capacity to repay a loan, a person's credit experience, the value of the property being financed, and the type of mortgage.

The product offerings, along with the level of service and support provided, are the primary factors in marketing our products to the mortgage brokers, who in turn sell them to their borrowers. While mortgage brokers are always looking for wholesalers who offer the most attractively priced products, the level of support provided to them is an important decision in their selection of a wholesaler.

Once the loan is created, it is then sold in the secondary market to investors. The secondary market facilitates the buying and selling of mortgages and helps ensure there will be an available supply of mortgage money.

Success in the mortgage business requires the talent and adroitness of constantly maintaining the delicate balance of satisfying our multiple constituencies and stakeholders, each with its own set of conflicting interests and needs. It also means that mechanisms need to exist to maintain familiarity with the changing needs and desires of each set of customers.

Industry Tenure – Measured by Cycles Survived

The financial services industry, especially the mortgage industry, is particularly susceptible to economic cycles and events. Traditionally, the mortgage business rides the economic and interest rate cycles, creating periods of boom and bust.

When interest rates decrease, there is a great rush to refinance existing mortgages and take advantage of increased home affordability. During these times, the industry races to expand its capacity to meet the demand. The hiring frenzy in a limited labor pool translates into extraordinary income opportunities for even clerical staff. Conversely, as the cycle turns and interest rates climb, the industry responds with a blizzard of pink slips. Mortgage industry veterans tend to describe their tenure in cycles survived, as opposed to years of service.

In addition to longer-term cyclical activity, world and national events exert influence on mortgages. Events such as the September 11, 2001, terrorist attacks and the collapse of the Asian economy in 1998 deeply affected the mortgage industry and secondary markets.

Beyond the longer-term economic cycles, mortgages and interest rates are actively traded, and the prices for these products change hourly. Try to imagine the risk management procedures that must be in place to deal with a 30-year fixed loan, when its underlying value may change on an hourly basis. Even companies like ours, which sell these loans quickly after they are produced, are still exposed to substantial market interest rate risk for up to several months, as marketable pools of loans are accumulated.

A characteristic of financial services is the perception by the general public that the industry is more of a public utility than a capitalistic enterprise. Perhaps this perception is a vestige of early medieval times when money-lending, an activity essential to the development of capitalism, was regarded as shameful gain, or filthy lucre. There seems to be resentment – a public feeling that we are unfairly receiving compensation, essentially for handling their money. Government regulators, taking their cue from public sentiment, have zealously followed suit, using the lending industry as the brunt of an avalanche of consumer protectionist regulation. An excellent example is some of the features of the Real Estate Settlement Procedures Act (RESPA). RESPA expressly prohibits anyone from being compensated for referrals of mortgages. In addition, any fees that are charged in the loan process are highly regulated. Remuneration for services provided, a governing principle found in most other businesses, is prohibited by regulation in this industry.

Coexisting with Fannie and Freddie

Of all the unique aspects of the mortgage industry, perhaps the most notable is the existence of the Government Sponsored Enterprises (GSEs). Fannie Mae and Freddie Mac are companies that were set up by the federal government and that receive preferential funding, implicit and implied government guarantees on their outstanding debt, and preferred and nonexistent tax rates.

These companies were created and chartered to promote affordable homeownership. At the outset these companies provided an attractive vehicle for public sector funds to be channeled into a new and deep source of liquidity for the financing of homeownership. In addition, they brought standardization to a highly fragmented industry and provided a means to bring an end to discrimination in the lending process.

Given advantages that private sector companies could only dream about, the GSEs prospered dramatically. A standing joke inside the mortgage industry is that in its best year, the combined profits of the industry totaled $18 billion, with Fannie Mae and Freddie Mac accounting for more than $16 billion. Fannie and Freddie, with their governmentally granted advantages, clearly dominate the industry. Indisputably, they contributed greatly toward expanding homeownership in their early years of existence. Nevertheless, their current focus on EPS (earnings per share) and stock price has created significant concern in an industry beset by already low margins. It is not an uncommon perception that the GSEs are contemplating entering businesses beyond the purview of their charter that would use their sovereign advantages in competition with a highly regulated private sector. Lacking the advantages granted to the GSEs, private-sector companies that compete in these areas wouldn't stand a chance in head-to-head competition with them.

Constants: Change and the Drive Toward Efficiency

That the American dream is predicated on homeownership means there is a never-ending momentum toward enhancing the efficiency by which mortgage product is delivered to the public. Our elected officials realize that homeowners are happier, more content, and more productive citizens, and they are continuously looking for ways to increase the percentage of homeownership.

This huge demand has attracted many providers of the product, which in turn has created an enormous pool of talent constantly seeking more efficient ways to provide financing to homebuyers. The result has been an accelerated pace of competitive one-upmanship, compounded by the constant prodding of heightened government regulation. While all of these conditions have benefited consumers – continuously improving their access to funds and lowering the cost of homeownership – it has created an environment of constant and fast-paced change in an industry where only those who can manage change and quickly adapt can survive.

Change is a constant in the financial services industry. There is a never-ending migration of the business toward a more efficient method of production. Change is driven not only by competing firms, but also by increasing regulation, as the government strives to push up homeownership rates. The communal desire to make homeownership more affordable has driven a tremendous amount of efficiency within the business. As I mentioned earlier, homeownership has expanded from 40 percent of the population to 70 percent and is likely to continue growing. In the end, those who cannot produce high-quality business efficiently at a very low cost simply won't make it.

The mortgage business is therefore a low-margin business with very small tolerance for error. You work like the proverbial dog to make a nickel, but if you take your eye off the ball for a moment, you lose a dollar. Thus, there is an ever-present need to create a repetitive and accurate system to do as much of the required work for you as possible. The company that creates the system that does the greatest volume of accurate work – with the greatest efficiency – wins.

The drive toward efficiency, already an intrinsic aspect of the industry, will intensify as margins decrease. In the purchase of a home, a large portion of the total purchase price is unrelated to the actual purchase price of the house itself, but rather is spent on ancillary services and closing costs: the realtor's commission, title insurance, escrow, the mortgage broker, the appraiser, inspectors, and insurers, each one's team of salespersons, and so on. The financial services industry, a recipient of a large portion of these ancillary costs, will be called upon to tighten its belt. To compete successfully in the mortgage business will require companies to find or create solutions that squeeze the cost out of this process.

E-Mortgage: Technology and the Industry's Future

Our company's approach to resolving the cost dilemma has been the technology route. Spurred on by the emerging electronic technology, the Internet, and the collapse of the Asian economy in 1998 – which was particularly devastating to the industry – we decided to invest in developing e-business solutions to automate loan-decision processes and integrate them into our back office procedures. We took the radical step of totally revamping our processes around the emerging electronic technology. In fact, we actually shut the company down for a period to integrate these new, fully automated processes. We succeeded in leveraging technology to become the first fully Internet-based wholesale lender to originate loans online exclusively.

As a result of revamping our business model to accommodate e-business technology, we have been able to cut our costs dramatically, allowing us not only to be more efficient, but also to pass these savings on to consumers.

After an interim period of adjustment due to the changeover to a Web-based business model and automated loan-decision systems, our company production volumes have returned to and surpassed the levels of business we did before the change. Our old business model required a staff of 1,300 employees. We can now accomplish the same work with just one fifth of that number, and we produce a substantially higher-quality product. Newly developed technologies offer the promise of enormous efficiencies. It is astonishing to think that not even two years ago it took almost five times the staff, or more than a thousand additional people, to do the same job we are doing today.

With the best of intentions – protecting consumers through new safeguards – regulators have unwittingly made an arduous process even more complex. As so often happens, well-meaning safeguards result in unanticipated consequences, often creating the exact opposite of the desired effect. So many additional disclosures and documents added as safeguards have resulted in obfuscation and complexity, which, in fact, has tended to further distance consumers from any understanding of what they are getting into. As a result the need will continue for a human being to sit with consumers at closings, explaining what is being agreed to, as they affix signatures and initials to document after document.

Every step in the process, up to that final signing, is undergoing automation. E-business innovations are being implemented to improve the cumbersome, labor-intensive, mortgage origination process. These advances reduce costs, cut down paperwork, and reduce the time it takes to fund the loan from months to days.

Automated underwriting systems (AU) and Internet loan origination have dramatically streamlined the application process. In the wholesale channel, mortgage brokers can submit their borrower's loan data to a lender's Web site and receive a decision, literally in seconds, the lender's decision being correlated to investor underwriting guidelines. Using a desktop loan origination software package (LOS), the broker can then upload the borrower loan file to the lender for completion. Comprehensive loan-decision platforms can manage, in real time, many loan-decision activities: product and rate distribution, loan registration and rate lock, automated underwriting, credit, appraisal, and mortgage insurance. AU systems were put to the test during the 2001 refinance boom. Originators were able to keep pace with sharp increases in loan volume, doing in minutes what used to take days. Real-time pricing and online interest rate-locking have enabled lenders to offer multitier pricing to brokers, and pipeline management tools have facilitated secondary marketing by making it easier to track, report, and hedge their production.

Current technology has the capability of providing mortgage brokers and their customers real-time online access to information located in our company's internal loan-decision systems. The technology, in essence, increases the quantity and the quality of information by eliminating the need for human intermediaries to be information providers. And as a result, a huge amount of time, effort, and expense is taken out of the process. The mortgage broker can respond to the consumer's needs and circumstances directly, and the process and experience are improved for both.

In mortgage applications the same documents shuttle among multiple parties in a notoriously time-consuming process. Technology could potentially save many millions of dollars in paperwork processing and handling costs. President Clinton signed the Electronic Signatures in Global and National

Commerce Act in October 2000. The law declared that signatures, contracts, and other documents in electronic formats are legally valid and binding in electronic commerce. The industry has high hopes that electronic signatures – digital codes for confirming the identity of parties in electronic transactions – will eventually become commonplace in online transactions. In addition, the steadily increasing bandwidth available at reasonable prices, coupled with the appropriate technology to use this bandwidth, will eventually allow for the elimination of the paper mortgage forever.

Adopting E-Technology and Managing Change

In the span of a few years the Internet and e-business solutions have had a profound impact on the financial services industry in the ways companies conduct business and their strategies for implementing technology. It remarkable to think that these technologies, still only in their nascent stages, have yet to fulfill their potential.

Adopting e-technology will be a major challenge for management if the corporate culture is inflexible and resistant to change. Companies must have a culture that not only recognizes change, but also actually embraces it. You can't bring everyone into a room every time change is required and tell them they are about to change. It's not practical and it just won't work. Instead, change must be a fundamental part of the culture. Change must be perceived as something positive, and every person in the company needs to be aligned with this attitude. Change is absolutely central to the way we do things and our ability to stay competitive. When we downsized, we were able to keep the best and the brightest, the people who recognize the value in change and view it as exciting and positive.

How do we recognize good change and bad change? This is where the talent and ability of the staff and, in particular, the corporate leadership weigh in. When presented with a change, we must go through the risk/reward and return-on-investment analysis involved in adopting that change. We put a lot of effort into identifying new technologies and new ways of doing business. If we don't have a clear vision, we will run tests in small markets to see whether there is a real long-term benefit to that particular process or technology. We don't allow things to catch up to us and hit us from behind. Instead, we are constantly looking for the better way, the better processes.

E-Business Facilitates Hiring the Best and Brightest

To have the best opportunity for survival and to ensure we possess the highest levels of talent and ability, we need to improve the way we recruit new people into the financial services business. Typically, we have hired most aggressively among the clerical levels, allowing them to train in the business and work their way up through the management ranks. This practice is outdated in today's highly specialized and sophisticated environment. Our business is becoming very complex, so we must make sure we hire the brightest people and train them to participate effectively in this complex industry. You can hire a smart person and teach him the mortgage business, but you can't hire someone who knows the mortgage business and make him smart. We can then use technology to leverage the capabilities of these brighter people, allowing us to keep costs low, even though the per-employee cost may be higher to attract these more qualified individuals. You simply can't have an army of marginally qualified people pushing paper anymore. Automation and technology must begin to handle the majority of the repetitive clerical functions, freeing a more talented and empowered staff to deal with more challenging tasks.

Our company has had great results with psychological profiling and testing. We now prepare psychological profiles on every one of our employees, both new and existing. We have developed psychological profile templates for each position in the company; this allows us to identify specific skills and profiles that best match each position. For example, a bright and charming person might not excel in sales because he or she is afraid of rejection. We find that people who are well-suited for performing credit reviews tend not be outgoing and gregarious, and generally are not the most ideal candidates for customer contact positions. We have put a concerted effort into developing these psychological profiles. Regardless of introversion or extroversion, we place the highest value on intelligence – our employees must be smart.

Traditionally the mortgage business, being as cyclical as it is, has been forced to rely on expediency in the hiring process. We would hire anyone with experience, stick that person at a desk, and forget about him or her until the cycle swung, and then lay them off. The leveraging effect that technology applies to the company's core talent base allows us to break this dismal cycle. Electronic technology's "scalability" gives us the capacity to gear up or gear down as cycles or volumes swing. We are freed from a great portion of the effects of the cycle, since the work once handled by an army of clerical staff is now fully automated. Without oversimplifying, the work increases and decreases could be handled by adding or removing an on online server.

We now hire bright people right out of college and train them ourselves in a highly developed training program. We have found that the quality of employee produced is much higher than we saw in the past under the old philosophy. We catch them before they have the opportunity to develop bad habits and opinions. This gives us the chance to ingrain in them our corporate culture and philosophy, so they grow up in business and in life thinking the way we do. Further, new employees experience a significant investment made in them by the company and develop a greater affinity for and loyalty to the company. Again, it is important to build a culture in which everyone in the company works together as a family, sharing the same attitude, vision, and goals. We have been able to build a cohesive, functioning organization aligned to a corporate culture conducive to achieving our goals.

Bright People Don't Repeat Mistakes

Working on Wall Street was one of the great molding events in my life. I was surrounded by incredibly capable and intelligent people. Everyone there is concentrated well to the right on the bell curve, in both capability and intellect. One of the most profound things I learned there is that intelligent people, even though very young, can in a short time become experts in their field. Bringing together a group of very capable, very motivated, and very intelligent people and providing them the right direction, tools, incentive, motivation, and vision will invariably get you to the finish line.

That idea is by far the most important element of my own leadership style. I bring in the best people I can find, send them in the direction they need to go, set the parameters, and create incentive and motivation for them. Once I've done that, I step back and let them do their thing. Very bright, intelligent, and motivated people don't like to be micromanaged; instead, you need to give them running room, so as not to inhibit their ability to create and produce. In some cases this even means giving them room to make mistakes. People learn a lot from their mistakes, and bright people don't make the same mistakes twice.

To successfully manage a company you must first build a culture of integrity, hard work, efficiency, and fiscal responsibility within the company. These elements must exist as a culture. People don't respond to mandates and projects as much as they respond to the cultural setting. Cost-cutting programs are ineffectual because as soon as the program is over, costs will rise again until the next program. Instead, you must set your objectives out as a cultural initiative. And the leader must set the example. Obviously, a cost-efficient culture will never propagate if the CEO berates an employee over office supplies as he climbs into his limousine on his way to the golf course. CEOs need to display the same degree of fiscal restraint they ask of their employees. This fosters respect and loyalty, as well as superior work – perhaps beyond what the employee perceives his or her capabilities to be.

Staying Focused

A major problem in business is a lack of focus. In the 1960s and 1970s all of the business schools were preaching vertical integration – controlling the process from cradle to grave. Perhaps that was the right idea for the time, but for today's business culture this is certainly not universally applicable, if at all. For many companies, what is really needed is to focus on one thing and do that one thing incredibly well.

Our company used to be in the retail business and the direct-to-consumer Internet business, and our entire system of regional branch offices handled our wholesale business. We found that it was too much of a distraction to try to run three completely different businesses, even though they were selling the same product. The technology is not fungible enough to deal with those different constituencies. To run a retail branch office, you need a terrific network. To run a Web site you need a great Web-enabled system. And then to run our wholesale business, process-flow technology is all-important. Not only is that a lot to invest in, but it also requires many different areas of expertise and management skill. In our case, we decided to shut down the retail and Internet direct business, and doing so has made a tremendous difference. It has allowed us to become extremely capable and successful at our core business, as opposed to marginally successful in three related businesses.

The ability to retain focus and avoid distractions proved to be critical when our company was presented with what, on the surface, looked like a golden opportunity.

One of the largest companies in the country came to me and said that they wanted out of one of their businesses. They offered us their retail business. It was very tempting, but I decided to turn it down out of fear of spreading ourselves too thin. They then came back and offered to pay us $8 million for us to take their company! While this at first sounded like an excellent offer, after we finished the analysis of how much it was going to cost our business in terms of distraction and growth slowdown, we realized it just wasn't worth it. In the end we passed on the deal, and within six months, our company was making far more money than that opportunity could ever have created for us. For us, that ability to stay focused, while difficult at the time, clearly proved to be a crucial factor in making the right decision.

On Leadership: Present and Future

You tend to gather skills as you go through life. Every experience, both good and bad, is a component of the total package. I had my own business as a teenager. I put myself through school. My educational background is in technology and accounting. From there I went into public accounting and had the chance to see how a variety of businesses worked. I then spent several years overseas, running businesses in an almost laboratory-like environment, where I had the opportunity to become involved in every aspect of running sophisticated businesses at a very young age. This experience also forced me to learn to manage and motivate a wide variety of people – people who were none too happy to be managed by some American "kid" who knew nothing about them, their culture, or their business. I have had varied experiences and education, but it has all come together in my current business. I draw upon all of my education and experience in operating our business. Certainly, a broad experience base provides a high degree of resourcefulness that is of great importance in managing a business in an industry that is as fast-paced as ours. I look across the business at my peers and I see a great variety of people. The financial services industry really does bring together multiple disciplines. There are some characteristics that some of the more successful leaders in our business share:

❏ *Competitiveness:* The desire to win drives continuous improvement in the products and processes.

❏ *Creativity:* There is a need for constant reinvention of the business to create a unique presence in a highly commoditized market.

❏ *Charisma:* One of the cornerstones of leadership is the ability to get and keep people motivated.

- ❏ *Discipline:* This is the ability to stay focused and avoid costly distraction. It's seeing important endeavors through to the finish.

- ❏ *Intellect:* Ours is a business with complex and constantly changing products and processes.

- ❏ *Multitasking ability:* We need the ability to simultaneously focus on diverse disciplines. You have to be able to walk out of a meeting with an aggressive salesman into a meeting with regulators without skipping a beat.

It is the combination of a variety of talents – along with strong leadership qualities – that leads to success. I tell anyone who is in a position of management, especially in a growing business: All of the technical skills that got you to where you are now have little bearing on what will make you successful going forward. Management skills are usually not taught to newly promoted managers. This is a huge failing in business. These shortcomings are exacerbated at each level of promotion; thus the realization of the dreaded "Peter Principle," where a once-capable employee is promoted to a level of incompetence. Successful survivors of the process are those who were able to assimilate management capability through experience, training, and observation and who possess the creativity to combine these qualities to deal with the unexpected.

Once you have achieved any degree of success, it is important to keep your edge. As business changes, the demands of management and leadership will inevitably change. These changes will require that you continue to expand your skill set beyond what you currently possess. Like any successful person, you must constantly critique yourself and your business. You can always do better. If you are not relentlessly self-critical, someone will sneak up and pass you by. Constantly look for better ways to do things because there will always be a better way; you never really are the very best. Someone is always performing some aspect of your business better than you are.

You have to stay in touch with your markets and your customers. Peter Lynch used to say he determined which stocks to buy by walking through a shopping mall. In our business we have to do the same thing. Americans are continuously buying houses. What are they going through? What do they need? What can you bring to them, and how can you present it to them in the most desirable fashion? I require that all management personnel, including the administrative staff, regularly accompany our sales staff on sales calls. I never fail to return from a round of sales calls without many revelations and ideas about our company and how we can improve.

While constant attention must be paid to what is going on in the core marketplace, you also need to pay that same close attention to the finance and technology world. Financial structures, debt and capital opportunities, and risks are constantly evolving, as is the cast of players in that world. Generally, the first company to take advantage of new financial structuring opportunities gets the best execution, and you can often benefit by knowing where the "deals" are. From the financial engineering aspect, raising capital from both the public and private markets will become more important, and as a result, CEOs will have to understand each element of these processes. Leaders in this business will require a working knowledge of more skills than ever before.

You must know exactly what technology is capable of doing, as opposed to what it is already doing. As a CEO, you will have to truly understand the technology yourself. It simply won't do anymore to call the CIO and tell him you want him to get your company onto the Internet. Your technology employees are not the best-suited to put out marketed-oriented pieces, and without involvement of all the different disciplines within the business, a very expensive initiative is doomed to failure. We will have to start dealing with enhanced levels of technology, as it clearly works. We will have to learn it, embrace it, and master the process of determining how to make a positive investment.

Ultimately, you must select and allow the technology to lead your business to new levels.

To lead successfully you must be confident. There is a huge difference between confidence and ego. You find a lot of middle managers with big egos, but you find a lot of leaders who are very confident. Confidence must be earned and learned and is generally incompatible with ego. As a CEO you will also have to recognize the need to surround yourself with better and brighter people. Keeping these higher-caliber people motivated, interested, and loyal to the business will provide a constant challenge. The business will continue to become more and more commoditized, so you will have to constantly maintain pressure not only on yourself, but also on the company, to become more and more efficient and look for better ways of doing things. The financial services industry will have to be very comfortable with moving forward, and as a result, the leader will not only have to be comfortable with it, but also be the inspiration for progress.

Specific Demands of the Mortgage Business

In our business several areas need focus. We are becoming a more regulated industry. There will be more government regulation, and business leaders will need to understand that. We deal in 50 states and multiple municipalities within each state. The leaders in the industry will have to understand the impact and limitations this granular regulation creates.

While I've already beaten the technology drum pretty hard, what drives it is the need to become ever more efficient. There is no doubt that the low-cost producer in any business will always have a distinct advantage, but in our business, the combined weight of competition and social mandate creates a frenetic race to lower costs.

There will continue to be a demand for greater balance sheet strength. The history of the financial service business has shown that as a product line matures, the business tends to gravitate to those with the most efficient means of attracting capital. So far, the capital markets have been efficient sources of capital, but deep pockets will eventually win. This concept has driven the tremendous consolidation in the banking and prime mortgage businesses and will be a force in all other financial product areas. Clearly, the most efficient sources of capital are the GSEs. We will be required to create ways to tap their tremendously efficient sources of capital.

Each industry has its own distinct set of challenges. While the difficulties each business leader faces may be different, many of the responses to these challenges are essentially the same. The financial service industry's product is the most basic of all – money. Everybody knows about money and has opinions and ideas about it. The formulas for making and manipulating money will constantly evolve, and the role of the financial services industry is to institutionalize these formulas and processes and turn them into products. Thus there will never be a simple answer to the question, "What's new?"

A leading innovator in the field of mortgage e-business, Scott McAfee, president and chief executive officer of WMC Mortgage Corporation, is frequently sought for speaking engagements and quoted often in media publications regarding mortgage industry issues.

Before assuming his current post in 1997, Mr. McAfee was president and CEO of Spring Mountain Group. With Security Pacific National Bank, as executive vice president in charge of all consumer lending and leasing, Mr. McAfee increased profitability in this group from $8 million to more than

$416 million in net annual earnings. He also was chief financial officer of Paine Webber Real Estate Securities.

In 1992 Mr. McAfee was named one of American Banker*'s "Top 40 under 40." He has served on the board of First Franklin Financial and on the advisory boards of TRW, GMAC Residential Funding, and PMI. Currently he is a board member of the Mortgage Bankers Association of America.*

THE CREATIVE MANAGEMENT OF STRATEGIC RELATIONSHIPS FOR LONG-TERM SUCCESS

EDWARD G. MCLAUGHLIN

Paytrust

Cofounder and Executive Vice President

Maintaining Focused Creativity

My management style is one of focused creativity. We are in a segment of the financial industry that is constantly challenged to reinvent and improve how we interface with our customers to deliver critical financial services. In the midst of all of the technical opportunities and innovations presented to our organization, we need to be vigilant in maintaining a tight focus on our core business objectives and our customers' needs and desires. By holding true to these guides, everyone in the organization – whether they are answering phones, working on a development project, or working with our partners – is able to understand how their activities build to the company's ultimate objectives. There is a great need for creativity and innovation, but it must be firmly anchored, or the organization's focus will be lost.

Keeping this focus without stifling creativity requires a clearly defined destination. You must know where the company needs to go, and the entire team must understand what they are setting out to accomplish. Once the ultimate destination is understood, then creativity can be unleashed, because there is a simple test every idea must pass: Is this moving us toward where we need to be? Blind alleys, erroneous assumptions, and other stumbles on the path simply become part of the learning process, providing course corrections along the way.

The life span of specific technologies is relatively short, but the needs, requirements, and desires of our customers are ongoing. It is easy to get caught up in the frenzy of the moment and lose sight of the future of the industry. If you simply create a product and leave it out there, despite getting useful feedback from customers, you are just refining a product frozen in a period of time and may miss the macro changes in the business environment. It is essential to have an environment in which your employees are comfortable enough to question the underlying assumptions of your products and to introduce suggestions and drive change.

In a rapidly changing market such as ours, the only truly sustainable competitive advantage is the ability to innovate. A clearly articulated focus will provide the parameters to unleash the creativity within in the organization and deliver the significant discontinuous innovations that drive the business forward.

Empowering and Inspiring Employees

In our business the employee base is the primary asset of the company. The products we deliver and the services that support them are the direct results of the intellect, motivation, and productivity of our employees. Maximizing this asset is the essential challenge to make a business thrive. The leadership of the company must establish straightforward objectives and create the necessary metrics to determine whether the goals are being met. Employees also deserve immediate feedback and long-term rewards for meeting – and exceeding – these goals.

Organizations often break down not because they have the wrong employees, but because these intelligent and (generally) well-meaning individuals literally are not sure what to do and are unclear as to how their activities are ultimately relevant to the business objectives. You have a responsibility to clearly delineate the corporate objectives and make sure employees truly understand their role in achieving them.

One of the primary rules in business is that no one ever works against their compensation plan; yet employees are sometimes faced with rewards that run counter to the company's stated objectives. No matter how grand the vision or how precise the market analysis, the employee rewards system must be carefully and completely aligned with the goal, or the organization may literally end up working against itself.

To truly surge ahead in a competitive, innovation-based market, clearly defined objectives, measures, and rewards are absolutely necessary, but simply not enough by themselves. Excellence cannot be achieved without passion, and creating enthusiasm in the business starts at the top. You must truly believe you are doing something important, that this is valuable to your customers – even that it has the potential to change the fabric of your industry. If you believe it, the rest of the company will come along with you. You must express your belief through constant communication, articulating why this mission is important and why the chosen approach will succeed. This sense of mission can inspire employees to stretch themselves, pushing the organization and maximizing the return on investment in this asset.

I am constantly selling my vision and myself to my employees. This helps inspire – and therefore empower – our employees. An empowered employee executes. Regular interaction is the most essential part of this sale. I interact with groups and individuals face-to-face as much as possible. If people believe they have input into the focus and direction of the company, it is easier for them to buy into it. They must not feel it is being pushed on them, but that they have a personal share in the development and ultimate success of the plan.

Another key to successful organizations is constantly working to place employees in their "power zones," matching their skills, experience, and personalities to the tasks for which they are best suited. Individuals often desire, or are pushed into, roles that are a mismatch with their personalities or current capabilities. Placing them in roles in which they are ill-prepared or incompatible is a disservice to the employee, their coworkers, and the company.

Teams are much stronger if they contain people with different approaches, perspectives, and skill sets. If people are assigned to roles that fit their specific qualities, then the team will be that much more effective. Finding the right blend of people and building the team is always an ongoing challenge, with the ever-present risk of having a bad hire you will have to correct later. I have found the best source of candidates is always personal references and referrals from your current employees. Peers understand who is good to work with and who is not, and will try to get the winners on their teams.

Assessing Risks and Thriving on Change

Knowing how to take the right risks is essential to success. You can never build a business without taking significant risk; the key is mitigating those risks. When you reach an inflection point, where a critical decision for the business must be made, you must be sure that as much relevant information has been gathered as possible, and you make what you believe to be the optimum choice based on that universe of information. Because there is never a complete set of perfect information available, after the decision has been made, you must create a method to check back on it. As you enter further into the risk phase, you are still monitoring the external factors that may affect the information you based your decision on. People get in trouble when they make what appears to be an optimal decision, but do not constantly evaluate the status of the decision while it is in motion.

A severe economic downturn does directly affect the risk assessment of potential business opportunities. We are now more careful in choosing what projects to take on; we now have a much higher threshold for projected success and more rigorous incremental testing. But even in down times, you cannot stop making your product better – in fact, constant improvement is mandatory to create more value for the business. As long as you maintain a stable base in your core business, you must keep innovating and be in position to take advantage of the next upswing.

The state of the economy does not necessitate a different management style. You must always be careful about managing your resources and be sure you can provide a cost-effective service for your customers. You must also always be focused on supporting the customers you have, especially when new ones are scarce. From a product perspective, what a downturn does emphasize is the need to not get too far ahead of your customers, and to make sure your products are focused on their core business drivers, rather than on more strategic objectives.

If you've positioned your company to thrive on change, you'll be flexible enough to be successful despite the ups and downs of the economy. From the beginning we wanted to make sure we had a rock-solid recurring revenue stream to help insulate us from wild changes in the marketplace. We then try to take advantage of the changes in the marketplace that our partners are responding to. For example, our partners Citibank and American Express were initially focused primarily on attracting customers to their Internet sites. Now the focus is more on retaining customers and leveraging the online relationships they have already established – improving account retention and figuring out how to increase revenue from these customers.

You must make sure you are orienting your products according to the strategic objectives of the customer. You must be aware of the changes in the market and align your product to fit in to these changes. Every change is an opportunity.

Focusing on Customer Needs

Generating consistent and open communication with customers is essential to ongoing success. We emphasize getting a lot of information out of our customer-support networks and making necessary incremental improvements to the product. However, one of the things you must be very careful about is not talking only to those who already use your product. If this happens, you may end up completely orienting your product toward those who already are using it, missing any additional and perhaps larger potential markets. We try to achieve a balance of working closely with our customers, and also allowing our very strong technological group and R&D group to spend a lot of time thinking about discontinuous innovations that are not yet on the market. They try to assess the areas of the market that have friction and devise solutions, ones that the customers themselves may not have considered. The partner companies we work with also give us feedback as to what their objectives are and what we can do to help them achieve these objectives. There must be a balance between these streams of input.

I keep my edge on what the customers want by constantly learning about and from the customers. You have to understand what they are looking for, while studying what the competition is doing. Once you understand what the competitors are doing, you must cross-fertilize and blend ideas to create a new product. You have to understand your challenges, while looking at successful companies in other industries to understand what you can do to succeed.

Customer service is fundamental to our business. We provide a means for customers to pay their bills, and if they have any questions or concerns, they must feel comfortable asking us a question. We have our own customer service team and manage our call center in-house. This allows our customers to call anytime, day or night, with questions and concerns. You must also have strong escalation policies. That the customer has reached someone is not enough. You hope the initial contact can handle 90 percent of the problems. Then you must deal with the remaining 10 percent, by escalating them to an engineering group or to the proper department.

We have found that customer support is as fundamental to the business as the initial marketing campaigns that generated the accounts. We recognize that no one really wants to have to call the hotline, and it is expensive for us to handle these calls. We've tried to make it more convenient for our customers by putting as much information as possible online at their fingertips. By allowing the customer to self-serve, we both increase satisfaction and lower their costs. For example, in our pilot phase we received many calls from people who had forgotten their password. By enabling a password retention service online, we weeded out some of the calls to our call center and made it more convenient for our customers. We continue to see strong returns through a constant emphasis on identifying our customers' issues and making the solution as efficient as possible.

Looking to the Future

The financial services industry will change a great deal over the next few years. One of the most common things we've been seeing is that businesses are trying to cross-sell and expand their lines of business. Banks are trying to link with insurance companies; card companies want to start stock-trading; mortgage companies want to offer you checking – everyone seems to be driving multichannel. You will see more organizations expanding their product offerings to customers, which they try to justify through the cost efficiencies of trying to sell everything to the same customer base. The customer has relationships simultaneously with five or six different financial institutions, and each is trying to be the dominant provider of financial services.

The critical question in this category expansion is this: If a consumer has a mortgage with an institution different from their insurance, are they truly interested in combining everything with the same institution, or do they see a benefit from segmenting their relationships? The theory of monolithic financial service integration is powerful and seductive, but yet to be truly proven in the market.

Online interaction is increasing rapidly, as well, opening up what may be an ideal avenue for financial cross-sell. Banks used to attempt cross-sell by simply putting more glossies in the branches and hoping people would pick them up off the rack.

Card companies would stuff more offers in their envelopes. Now, with online bill payment, you can get your customers coming to your site frequently, and you can have more targeted information available to present them. There is a new dialogue developing online between customer and financial institution. Companies can now effectively enter new financial services markets, enabled and aided by the Internet.

The key to penetrating these new markets is to leverage existing relationships and a high degree of personalization to deliver targeted incremental product offers. The service providers must factually demonstrate to their customers the worth of their services and ideas. Simply presenting a "supermarket" of services does not generate a compelling enough value proposition for the consumer to change entrenched behaviors. The lynchpin of the message must be personal benefits obtained by increasing the level of the relationship between the customer and the institution.

The potential danger of combining all of one's financial services is always a concern in consumer surveys. People fear a big brother having total control over their finances. At times, consumers appear to intentionally separate their financial lives across different companies. If people feel information is being used inappropriately – that it is being leveraged too aggressively – they react negatively. This potential reaction must be mitigated by strong messages of the benefits and conveniences of integration, paid off by the quality of the services. The additional services can also be presented as an "opt-in" capability, such as automatically feeding personal information into an online calculator to assist in financial planning. By presenting the new product as customer or membership benefits and clearly demonstrating the benefits of integration, online channels may prove to be the ultimate delivery channel for multicategory financial product sales.

Edward McLaughlin is cofounder of Paytrust, Inc., and has served as executive vice president since the company's inception in October 1998. Mr. McLaughlin oversees the company's product direction, strategic relationships, marketing, and long-term vision.

Before founding Paytrust, Mr. McLaughlin was executive vice president of marketing at Logic Works, and before that, director of information tools at Actium, a leading systems integrator; manager of EDI Services at Information and Financial Services, a leading software and services company; and corporate services analyst at Industrial Valley Bank.

Mr. McLaughlin holds a Bachelor of Science degree in finance and decision science from the Wharton School, University of Pennsylvania.

BRINGING THE WORLD TOGETHER THROUGH COMMERCE

MICHAEL P. DUFFY

Paymentech, LP

President and Chief Executive Officer

Electronic Payment Services

If, as the song says, "Money makes the world go 'round," then the financial services industry powers the globe. Our vision for the industry is quite simply to bring the world together through secure, reliable payment solutions, a vision we strive to realize through delivering innovative and valuable services to our customers.

Electronic payment services allow merchants or businesses to accept bank automated clearinghouse (ACH) payments, as well as any card payments from any major card brand. Through the ACH system, merchants can access funds directly at their banks. The types of payments that can be supported include Visa, MasterCard, American Express, and Discover, as well as stored value cards, electronic checks, and private-label cards.

In addition, we operate back-end systems that assist our customers in managing the payment transaction life cycle, which includes providing reporting, data files, and dispute resolution systems.

Following a Road Map for Success

Leading a company that enables merchants to receive payments for the products and services they provide is an exciting and challenging responsibility. A constantly changing economy, coupled with technology advancements, creates an environment in which a company's ability to adapt and respond to the current marketplace, while still preparing for future demand, may be the single most important factor for long-term growth and success. There will most certainly be periods of economic downturn, when consumers tighten their belts and growth slows, just as there are periods of economic growth in which a company may struggle to keep up with the increased demand for service. In both cases, maintaining a disciplined and focused attention to the principles and strategies on which you have built your business becomes even more important as you work to retain and grow your business.

Our company has weathered many economic climates since our formation in 1985, and we still have managed to outpace the growth of our industry as we have acquired complementary businesses and grown organically through adding new products and services. Our company began with fewer than 50 people, as an afterthought of an established financial institution looking for ways to address the needs of their business customers. Now, with a workforce of more than 1,400 talented employees servicing hundreds of thousands of merchant clients in the United States, Canada, and beyond, merchant services is no longer an afterthought, but a dynamic and profitable service industry in its own right.

It is astounding to measure the phenomenal growth, both in transactions processed and in merchant categories served, in our quest to unite the world through electronic payments. But knowing where you want to go is only the first step. We need a roadmap to guide our path and identify the landmarks along the way. When we developed our strategic roadmap, we kept it simple. There are three basic strategic planks on which we anchor the company. Each year we review the planks to ensure they still belong on our road map.

Our first plank is following the sun. It is our international strategy, which is more of a push than a pull. We will be where our customers need to be and support the products that our customers require. If it is important for our customers to grow their business globally, we will expand our services so that our relationship continues to grow. If our customers need to offer new methods of payment to their consumers, we will develop payment types and establish relationships with vendors that allow us to meet our customers' needs. We take our cues from our customers, and make our investments in technology, infrastructure, and other resources accordingly. We will be where the sun is – where our customers are.

The second plank on which we establish priorities and build our business is conquering the category. We recognize that the financial services needs of a national catalog business are significantly different from the needs of a neighborhood pizza chain, and we develop our products and services with many vertical markets in mind. Likewise, we develop our marketing and product development strategies to leverage our strengths and the perceived opportunities in each of our vertical markets or categories. Our goal is to continue to dominate the categories in which we are strongest, and to become stronger in our weaker categories, all the while realizing we will not try to be all things to all people.

Our third plank is taking care of business. This has to do with investing in our people, the best in the business, and thereby supporting our customers. The most important responsibility of the management team is to make sure each employee is equipped to do his or her job as efficiently and effectively as possible. Our employees are encouraged to pursue training opportunities that enrich their capabilities. Internal peer-to-peer and corporate recognition programs reward top-performing employees on a quarterly basis.

But all of these important employee programs cannot alone produce the passion and commitment we need to take care of business. It is the job of the executive management team to inspire passion through powerful communication and consistent visibility. It is easy to fill a company with employees who will simply punch the clock and give a good day's work for a good dollar. We challenge our employees to go the extra mile by showing them a goal and providing an incentive in the form of a monetary reward if they reach this goal. As leaders we ask nothing more of our employees than we expect of ourselves.

While we rely heavily on the numbers to plan for future growth, these three strategies help us make sure the numbers we plan to achieve follow the guiding philosophy of the company. At the end of the day, we may not have planned to do something, but if it means strengthening our position for the future, then we must do it. Even though we have a roadmap, we sometimes have to take a left to go right. Sometimes the market dictates that you cannot just keep going straight.

Delivering a Real Value Proposition

Many in the industry have long categorized electronic payment processing as a commodity. Nothing could be further from the truth. For more than 16 years, we have proved that if you deliver a better or more valuable service or product, customers will appreciate it and be willing to pay for it. We have learned that if our products meet the following simple criteria, our customers will recognize the value, even if it costs a little more.

❑ *Deliver service reliably and accurately:* Each of our products should perform like clockwork, providing the service our customers expect when they expect it.

❑ *Provide innovative and powerful product options:* Our customers are the leaders in their field, and they rely on us to keep them not only abreast but ahead of the trends. When we provide our customers with all the options, they can make smart decisions that grow not only their business, but ours, as well.

❑ *Support our products and services:* Quality customer support, expert consultation, and proactive training ensure our products and services don't simply operate; they really work for our customers.

Technology is also important, because when understood and used properly, it will give a big competitive edge. Millions of transactions occur every day. Our competition uses the conventional "big blue box" way, processing all of the transactions on large mainframes. But we are the first to employ a distributed processing technique in which we use a family of Unix-based direction processors to move critical transaction data. Our approach gives us greater flexibility to respond to changes in technology and to react to unexpected service or performance problems. Staying ahead of the technology curve requires not only the discipline to consistently reinvest, but also the vision to build a system infrastructure to support tomorrow's innovations.

You must always understand your value equation and stick to it. When your numbers are off, you cannot abandon your principles. Over time you will gain confidence that you have the right product and the right service.

Entrepreneurial Environment

Risk is essential to success. Some risks are worth tolerating a larger margin for error. Occasionally we have launched products and didn't get the immediate demand we expected. Nonetheless, we were convinced that, strategically, it was the right move. Upon reanalyzing the results, we are able to tweak the positioning and still achieve the desired return on investment. It takes discipline not to panic. If decisions are based on research and support the corporate strategy, the product will eventually succeed. A mantra we have is that no one will be shot for taking a measured risk or making a mistake, but you will be shot for covering it up.

In fact, we've had a few situations in which an employee's judgment led to a costly failure or mistake. In each case, the individual made a calculated decision based on the unique situation. That is a risk we are willing to take to promote an environment that nurtures entrepreneurial thinking.

Promoting a philosophy of innovation is a key to taking the right risks. We have a business council free of executives, made up of those out in the market and the sales force. It is their mission to identify and share trends; then the information is filtered to our executive council. If a trend is seen, we will know about it. Our best new products have come from the ideas of those in the field. That has been a key to our success. It's another way in which our entrepreneurial spirit impacts our business. We have a lot of people listening to the marketplace, and we have a lot of people listening to them.

Leaders Who Serve in a Team Atmosphere

Ultimately, it is the leadership team's responsibility to ensure the quality of the products and services your company provides. One of our mantras is "leaders that serve." We will not hesitate to roll up our sleeves to do the work. We are not a hierarchical company, and each employee is given the opportunity and is encouraged to understand the vision, mission, and goals of the company. We hold update meetings every 60 days to review the income statement, balance sheet, and overall corporate environment with our employees. This helps us reach our goals. All of our employees are on the same bonus plan, so if one person gets a bonus, all employees get a bonus. This ensures a team approach. This also makes it even more important for us to keep people informed about goals.

We also make sure that as we grow, we maintain our open-door, non-hierarchical environment. Our employees and managers are able to make the decisions that enable them to do their jobs and meet the needs of our customers. We have grown into a substantial company, but we are still nimble. Being smaller than the giants in the industry can help us attract better people who want to have a voice that will matter and that can change things.

As a company we also take our responsibility as a corporate citizen very seriously. We have adopted public schools near our offices so that our employees may volunteer time to tutor students during work hours. Additionally, we support many local and national charities through both financial gifts and the efforts of our employees. Our company has a responsibility to make money, but also to benefit the community around us.

But despite all of the hard work, we make sure we foster an environment where people can have fun.

Establishing Metrics for Measuring Success

To consider ourselves successful, we evaluate several targets, or metrics. The first type of target is financial: We must make our bottom line. When you report to your shareholders, you must be able to tell them their goals are your goals – even our bonus plan, which is a target-based plan. The bottom line is an excellent indicator of success. Bear in mind that in a softer economy, if you can grow your bottom line, you are doing a great job at managing your budget. We have been able to increase our margins during a lean economy.

We also establish operational targets related to the performance of special projects or initiatives. For instance, we established targets when building and launching our seamless international currency product that moves multiple currencies simultaneously. When we built this product, we knew what we wanted to accomplish, but we had to develop a plan for how to achieve our goal. The most important part of developing that target is evaluating your performance once you get there. While your grade may never be 100 percent, much can be learned from determining why you didn't hit your mark. Learning from shortcomings on one project makes you smarter and able to perform much better the next time you set a target. It's like setting a stake. In this industry, which focuses on what a company can do for the customer tomorrow, successfully launching products becomes even more important and helps build long-term customer loyalty.

Attrition is a major indicator of our success in satisfying our customers. As we build relationships with customers, we work to balance our strategic principles with pleasing our merchants.

Satisfying our customer base is still our top priority, and customer service is integral to remaining successful in this industry. We monitor calls into our service center, evaluating how quickly and effectively we are able to answer our customers' needs. For instance, we measure our abandonment rate – how often calls drop off the system before a customer service representative picks up.

As we have grown, the growth denominator has shrunk. This can be frustrating, so you must remind your team to keep the faith. "We are here for the long run" is the message we want to convey.

Future of Payment Processing

The Internet and Financial Services

The Internet had a tremendous impact on the financial services industry and will continue to affect it in the future. The Internet has not merely changed the industry by facilitating commerce, but more important by providing a medium and a means of moving data faster, more cheaply, and more securely.

It is no secret that the advent of the dot-com merchant changed the face of commerce. Adapting service models, pricing policies, and risk procedures to support the new-age merchant was critical to winning the business of start-up online merchants and entrepreneurs before they became recognizable brand names and profitable market leaders. Having established expertise in this industry from the outset, our company has been in position to continue to grow and excel in the market as the prevailing success model has changed to "brick and click," an integrated online and offline merchant with both a Web site and outlets. As a result we are able to service the total payment needs of our clients as they grow and evolve.

The Internet also plays an important role in the evolution of customer support. Web-enabled tools, such as knowledge-based information resolution applets and self-service account reporting, not only empower customers to access and use their data more effectively, but they also free resources for our support team from repetitive trouble-shooting tasks. An initial investment in network infrastructure pays off in the long-term benefits of informed and satisfied customers.

As exciting as the dot-com explosion has been, the ability to leverage the powerful Internet infrastructure as the primary communication and data delivery mechanism has dramatic implications. From speeding up the way new customers board our system and become active customers, to replacing multiple lease lines with more cost effective connections, the old industry standard will become obsolete. We benefit – and our clients benefit – from these applications of Internet technology.

Payment Internationalization and Emerging Payment Types

Quite simply, our large customers are learning that their businesses can no longer be run regionally, but must be run globally, and we are poised to support their international commerce needs. However, globalization presents great challenges, primarily because of the various new methods of payment that companies such as ours will have to support. When our customers expand their businesses overseas, they will encounter different currencies and methods of payment beyond simply U.S. dollars, MasterCard, and Visa. Globalization also means understanding payment customs and applying technologies to address the corresponding issues. In London, for example, debit payments were more accepted than traditional credit card payments, the complete opposite from the United States. As a result, for a merchant who wishes to be successful in

Britain, the ability to accept debit cards becomes a critical factor. We must be able to respond to that need.

As an international player we will have to understand and integrate new payment types into our regular methods of payment offering. We must be able to provide the full range of payment methods to whatever currency or region we plan to serve. This is one way in which we've positioned ourselves to take advantage of new opportunities and thrive on change in the marketplace.

The biggest opportunities for growth in the industry are in the emerging methods payment and new types of automated transactions. Consumers are looking for efficiencies in their daily lives. People are interested in paying their bills online or getting a soda from a vending machine using their cellular phone. Our industry is a great industry to join, and people have joined this great company because of our technological prowess and opportunity. The financial service business has tremendous opportunity.

Consolidation and Growth in the Industry

Over the next five years the industry will favor those who can adapt to the changing market. You will either consolidate or be left behind. It is better to be the consolidator rather than the company that is consolidated. Consolidations generate rapid growth and create opportunities, but can also be challenging. Blending corporate cultures, marrying technology systems, and creating a single-company approach takes time and the concerted effort of senior managers.

To survive the consolidation and take advantage of the opportunities for growth, we are focusing on servicing the customer. Service is paramount. There are varying degrees of service, depending on the customer. At first we gave everyone the Cadillac service, even those who bought a Buick. Now we vary our service levels. Second, you must understand your technological capabilities and have a good recipe for taking risk. Third, it all comes down to the people.

We have become a market leader not only because of what we offer our customers, but also because of the way we have changed the electronic payments processing world. We have helped revolutionize e-commerce; we have pioneered electronic payments in emerging market segments – utilities, insurance, telephony, and cable TV, for example – where automated payments have not been available before.

Michael P. Duffy was named president and CEO of Paymentech in 2000, following three years as chief operating officer. In overseeing overall technology and network services and sales, he was responsible for guiding the company's progression toward an integrated, enterprisewide infrastructure.

Mr. Duffy came to Paymentech in 1995 as the group executive of the company's direct response operations in Salem, New Hampshire. He was chief financial officer at Litle & Company from 1992 through 1995, when Paymentech acquired the firm. He previously served in financial management positions at Equifax Credit Information Services and Equifax Credit Bureau Marketing. In more than 15 years in banking, he has experience in accounting, sales, finance, and administration.

Under his leadership Paymentech has embarked on several community relations activities, including Project Outreach, in which Paymentech sponsors local elementary schools. Project Outreach allows Paymentech employees to volunteer their time to tutor students, work to improve the physical buildings of the schools, and help coordinate and attend field trips for the students. Paymentech also helps the school with grants, ensuring the students have the supplies and learning materials to make them successful in their studies. Mr. Duffy also serves on several association boards, the Leukemia and Lymphoma Society, and Asian American Hotel Owner Association (AAHOA).

Mr. Duffy holds a bachelor's degree in economics from the State University of New York at Albany and a master's degree in business administration from the University of St. Thomas in Houston, Texas.

OVER THE FENCE: A PEEK INSIDE A TOP-TIER CANADIAN FIRM

JAMES L. (JIM) HUNTER

Mackenzie Financial Corporation

President, Chief Executive Officer, and Director

Strength of the Canadian Financial Services Industry

The Canadian financial services industry is dynamic. Its growth in recent years has been healthy, and its prospects are exciting. The industry, like few others, exists on the cutting edge. It survives and pushes forward on the strength of cutting-edge technology, business management, and financial engineering.

Technology and business savvy change our industry by the day, and participants must innovate to survive. Everyone – our clients, our customers, our business partners, our competitors, other industries, and the general public at large – will be affected by this progress. In many ways the financial services industry is a steam engine, pulling others along with its many innovations.

As a business leader many enterprise-related parts to the financial services industry leave me thoroughly impressed. The industry has a history of profitability; it has great potential; and it has demonstrated an unwavering heartiness, even in dark days. It is not a coincidence that shareholders are drawn to Canadian financial services firms. The sector is well-financed; the decision makers have been bold, smart, and for the most part correct; and there are few industries that rival its blue-chip spirit.

Looking forward, the greatest challenge for our industry will be one that has challenged us for as long as there have been investors – namely, intangibles. For example, when equity markets decline, there is little you can do. As the leader of a company you accept those factors, assess them, and move on to deal with them as quickly and effectively as possible. These are the times when you prove your mettle.

Businesses that don't prepare for economic turbulence will invariably struggle when it hits. Mackenzie goes beyond merely preparing for the worst. Our business plan dictates that we prosper in downturns, as well as in times of economic growth. Being a strong company only when the economy and those around you are strong is simply not good enough.

Financial strength that is not crippled in a down economy can be used as a platform for future growth. Looking forward, every business in our industry will face a down market – this shouldn't be a surprise. So test your business model; determine whether it will survive a down economy; and, if not, outline a strategy that builds resources in good times for growth opportunities in bad times.

In tough times financial strength will usually separate the winners and the losers. As your competitors falter or consolidate in pursuit of scale, maintain a business-as-usual stance, or as close to one as you can muster. Rather than using "the poor economy" as an excuse, use it as an opportunity.

Our industry is a tough one in difficult times. Few other industries face the magnitude of pressure we face. Financial services clients simply cannot bear excuses. As a whole our industry has the financial future of most Canadian families in our hands. At Mackenzie, we have tried to live up to our motto and charge ourselves with the responsibility of "building financial independence." This is a challenge that we and our industry cannot take lightly.

When times are tough, the resulting stress on investors and our workforce can be immense – leaders will surely bear some of this stress. Similarly, when financial products don't perform as well as investors would like, questions will be asked and demands made – leaders will never escape demands and questions.

Pressures, demands, and inquiries are inherent to our industry; you can pretty much set your watch by them. My advice: Do your best to be prepared for each; meet them with honesty and a plan; and remember them, because they will surely come up again.

The Function of the CEO: Planning and Motivating

The most exciting aspects of my job have to do with the people. This industry attracts bright, innovative, and entrepreneurial thinkers who interact in an atmosphere that is as challenging as it is satisfying. I work with many people who are more talented than I. As a business leader, there isn't a better situation imaginable.

My management style encourages everyone to take a kick at the can – every idea is up for thoughtful debate. Fortunately, I have a collegial management team. Rather than muzzle our staff with a top-down style and rigid directions, we prefer to be part of the decision-making process, not the decision makers.

I believe Mackenzie is full of individual visions; experience tells me every one of our talented people has an idea of where they think the company should go. Together, these visions become a single one, and our talented team moves our company forward.

Whether it's an individual's employment proposal or an entire department's strategic plan, every idea should be met with encouragement. Every question should be met with more questions, and every individual should be motivated.

I would urge those who feel they need to *manage* from the top down to try something different: *Motivate* from the top down.

As you open the floodgates for ideas from your staff, think of them as puzzle pieces, each with a position that makes sense in the larger picture. The task of putting the puzzle together falls on the business leaders.

While multiple visions move a company forward, there are always fiscal considerations, industry developments, and other concerns at play. Often vision will have to take a back seat to reality because a company built solely on vision cannot survive – a lesson learned in record numbers during the dot-com crash.

Innovation

Virtually every plan should be built on innovation. This is especially true of financial services and other competitive industries in which the prospect of "new and improved" is king. In a competitive environment, you must innovate to thrive. If you fail to innovate, your competitors will see to it that you drown.

Mackenzie has a reputation for innovation. We take a long-term view and make constant investments in the systems, products, and developments we think we will need to remain competitive.

Year after year, we have introduced more innovative products into the industry than our competitors, a commitment that has driven our success. But we never rest on our laurels. True industry leaders look ahead, keep new products and services in the pipeline, and draft the blueprints for future revenue well before they are needed.

With input from my colleagues, I set plans to be executed well into the future. And as yesterday's vision becomes today's business plan, alterations are inevitable. What may have seemed like a good idea in the past may not be easily applied today – a reminder that flexibility is a must.

As plans become action, accountability, active management, and the timely completion of projects take the place of vision and foresight. Employees must stay on track; projects must be managed efficiently; and start-up costs cannot be allowed to destroy the existing business.

Mackenzie's project teams are diverse, made up of experts from various disciplines. This ensures that we continue to maximize the innovation, creativity, and skills of employees from every corner of our business, and that new ideas flow freely.

As CEO I monitor various elements of our new product cycle from start to finish, all the while ready to go back to the drawing board with corrections or to encourage those with new ideas. Even as exciting new business and new products come to fruition, I cannot afford to overlook innovation or new ideas; they are the cornerstones of future success.

A successful management team must have the potential capability to improve the financial status of the company. Mackenzie's officers spend 10 percent of their time discussing, planning and refining new development projects. If an idea is innovative, fresh, and potentially profitable, it will command attention immediately, not some time down the road.

As new ideas, innovations, and strategic plans come and go, organizations change – it's a reality in any industry. As changes occur make certain they don't impact the confidence of your employee base. If employees feel threatened by change, they are likely to be less productive.

Similarly, as changes occur, the threat of losing a job or facing the wrath of a heavy-handed manager will almost always have a stifling effect on your employees and ultimately the innovative spirit of your company. Conflict should be kept to a minimum, and you must allow room for honest mistakes. Conflicts can be avoided by driving employees toward specified goals. Even as those goals are altered, your staff will know what is expected and realize when they have missed or achieved their benchmark.

Some people have a fairly narrow view of their tasks. The best executives are often those who can broaden that view by explaining the tasks and expectations ahead, and painting the whole picture for their staff.

It is also valuable to be able to communicate both the positive and the negative aspects of specific responsibilities, while at the same time motivating an entire team to approach good and bad tasks with equal vigor. Executives must also prove they are game for the task at hand and anything change may bring. Roll up your sleeves; it sends a powerful message.

Ideally, there should be no difference in the professional treatment of different positions within a company. In this rite, communication is a powerful tool. Whether you are in good times, bad times, or times of change, or you are just maintaining the status quo, trust and open communication must extend throughout the company – top to bottom, bottom to top, top to top, and so on.

If you hold everyone in the same esteem – the employees, the executives, and the shareholders – everyone should feel a greater urge to work together. A team with a common goal will always be more powerful than a gang with scattered individual interests.

Defining and Measuring Success

Success is contagious. I learned most of what I know from colleagues and from my formal and practical business education.

Once you have gotten as much formal education as possible, align yourself to work with talented people. Talented people must have integrity, an innovative spirit, and interpersonal skills – attributes I find in my favorite colleagues and the people who teach me new skills and insights.

Preparation is another key to success. Assemble a structured team; put together a flexible plan; and get ready to make tough decisions in a variety of situations. Even if "the worst" never comes, you'll always be better off having prepared for it.

Be equally prepared during boom times, when it seems that improving the business is easy, and nothing can go wrong. Preparation requires that you don't go overboard, overspend, or hire irrational numbers of people. Business leaders must cushion their companies from the adverse effects of both the boom and the bust. Preparation often means not overextending yourself in good times.

There are many components to the success of a company. At Mackenzie success means making a difference to our customers; providing a fair return to shareholders; and most important, innovating and improving our business as a whole. Doing the right thing on multiple levels make us successful.

As an individual my success hinges on the interests of my people, my shareholders, and my customers. It is proved by my ability to say – with conviction – that I pleased as many of these groups as possible.

Sometimes your stakeholders' happiness – and therefore your success – will be delayed when short-term choices don't fall immediately in line with their interests. But the end goal is the overall satisfaction of a large and diverse collection of interest groups.

Accountability is critical. To ensure that your business is successful, create targets and pursue them. To ensure your own success, meet those targets. It is one thing to maintain a successful company with solid products. It's quite another to drive that company forward by finding new efficiencies, lowering costs, and raising customer service.

As a business leader, there will be risks in virtually all you do, but risk-taking is essential to success. Determining the right risk to take is an art. As a larger company Mackenzie can take larger risks than a smaller firm, but experience suggests that it's never worth sacrificing the well-being of your company.

Risks have pushed Mackenzie forward, but we have never been cavalier. By taking small, calculated risks, we can be sure that if we hit on four out of five, we will improve the business – but we also know that the one we miss will never be our downfall.

We have made a series of small, successful acquisitions, buying companies that share a common characteristic: They fit with our plan. And if they don't fit right away, we mold them. This principle has ensured that we never waver far from our long-term plan.

In an industry that lives and dies by the bottom line, uncertainty can be tough. However, there is no recipe for the perfect business plan. As I've said, have a plan, but welcome new ideas, be creative, embrace change, be flexible, take risks, and make revisions. Lastly, surround yourself with people who will question your plan again and again.

Ideas are improved by scrutiny, and so are you. Make sure there are five or six people around who could do your job. This will keep you sharp. Wise colleagues will teach you new lessons daily and become catalysts in your success.

The Successful Leader

To be a successful leader, you must work hard and be persistent. People will always throw roadblocks in your way – competitive pressures, business propositions, doubts. If you think you are right, keep pushing forward. Regardless of your industry, leadership is often a game of best guesses.

Ultimately, your success will often be determined by history. A string of knowledgeable, researched guesses and a reputation for good management will reflect favorably on you.

The world is too complex and changes too quickly to accurately predict and prepare for certainty down the road. I can't predict whether our company will be around in a hundred years. But I can say with some certainty that it's safe to look out 10 years or so, assuming our plans and visions stay flexible.

One thing I can say with some measure of certainty: If we build a rigid structure, it will shatter with the first major change. So we continue to set goals but never bank on them. Underlying themes power and alter every industry. Don't try to anticipate them and predict their effect. Instead, prepare for them and understand their effect.

At times these themes will combine with a particularly innovative player, good market conditions, or a strong economy, and a boom ensues. At other times, industry strife, reluctant consumers, or a recession can drag you down. Boom or bust, the winners and losers are separated by the flexible execution of their plans.

A plan is nothing more than a list of goals and a roadmap to reach them. Goals are created by vision and fulfilled by willing minds and skilled hands. When multiple visions combine to create better and more specialized goals, the result is innovation.

With goals, innovation, and a leader surrounded by free-thinkers, your chances for success become greater and greater. But in the end, whether you were truly successful is up to history to decide.

After graduating from the MBA program at the University of Western Ontario, Jim Hunter joined the public accounting firm Deloitte Haskins & Sells, qualifying as a Chartered Accountant in 1979. He spent 17 years with Deloitte in Toronto and in London, England, latterly as a senior partner in its financial services practice. He was elected a Fellow of the Institute of Chartered Accountants of Ontario in March 2000.

Mr. Hunter's first involvement with Mackenzie began in 1991 as an advisor to Midland Walwyn, Inc., a former Mackenzie investment. In September 1992 Mr. Hunter joined Mackenzie as chief financial officer and chairman of the Executive Committee.

In 1994 Mr. Hunter was appointed chief operating officer, and in 1997 chief executive officer. In addition to his responsibilities at Mackenzie itself, he serves as chairman of the MRS Group of Companies and is a director of Mackenzie Investment Management, Inc. in the United States. He is or has been an advisor or director of a number of public companies and charities and currently sits on the advisory board of The Richard Ivey School of Business, is a director of The Trillium Foundation, and is a director and Executive Committee member of the Investment Funds Institute of Canada.

NICHE MARKETING AND THE IMPORTANCE OF BEING OPPORTUNISTIC

RALPH H. CLINARD

Cardtronics

Chief Executive Officer

Finding a Niche

One significant key to success in business is finding a niche in the market. It is important to keep your eyes and ears open, because you just might find an unoccupied niche and be able to take advantage of it. For example, I was in credit-card merchant-processing services, setting up merchants to accept credit cards. By keeping track of trends, I learned that debit cards were very attractive to the service providers, because they could earn significant residuals on each transaction. I learned there was money to be made in debit cards in terms of cents per transaction. Heavy use of debit cards occurred primarily in businesses where the receipts were small, such as convenience stores, where the average receipt today is $3.50. In stores of that nature, people tend to use cash, and they come into convenience stores to replenish their cash.

In this manner I "followed the money" and started soliciting convenience stores for point-of-sale business. I noticed that the big chain stores were the only merchants that had cash machines, and that banks installed those cash machines. The mom-and-pop stores I was servicing couldn't compete with the big cash machines in the chain stores, and the point-of-sale device didn't give them the right ammunition, because people are uneasy about getting cash back in front of the clerk or other customers. So I became aware of a device called a scrip machine, which is a stand-alone device used just like a cash machine, except without the cash. Instead of dispensing money, the machine prints a receipt, which the customer redeems at the cash register.

I thought the scrip machine might be a good way for the small stores to compete, but I didn't like the designs that were available. Taking advantage of my engineering background, I set out to design a scrip machine. About 10 models later, I had one. That's what launched the company. We identified and capitalized on a niche in the Houston area.

We captured much of the Houston mom-and-pop market, and by 1996, we were doing big business in scrip transactions in Texas. We had 900 to 950 machines out in the marketplace that we designed, assembled, and sold or placed. When low-cost cash machines specifically designed for retail locations began to compete with our machines, we made the transition into the cash machine business. Many of the scrip machine accounts were converted into cash machine accounts.

In the early 1990s the local Pulse network in the Houston area embraced surcharging, before many other regions of the nation did this. Because we were able to place a surcharge on cash-back transactions, we had an advantage and a jump-start on competitors.

While being in the right place at the right time is important, you identify opportunities by being alert and seizing opportunities that become apparent through analysis of certain situations. You have to be perceptive enough to identify a need and capitalize on it before your competition does.

Growing the Business

Until recently we didn't pursue large corporate business, preferring instead to grow the business in a safe manner. We knew the best way to grow without risking a lot of capital, which we didn't have, was to expand the business one merchant at a time, instead of attempting to capture large chain accounts. Growing the business one merchant at a time allowed us to slowly develop a large customer base, and if we lost one customer, it was not a large percentage of our total business.

We knew it was time to look for an investor in 2001, when we got to a point where the future was bright, but we couldn't get there without capital. We knew we couldn't handle any more debt, but we were in a tremendous growth mode, so we searched for an investor or even a larger company that might want to buy us. In that process we investigated about half a dozen opportunities before we found the right one. We knew when we had the right one because 1) the investors were the same kind of people we were; 2) they were local; 3) they had 12 years of successful ventures; and 4) they had a lot of financial strength. Last but not least, we were pleased with what they paid us for the share they purchased. They are a talented and capable group of people who we feel will help us grow the business to greater heights.

The investment in 2001 gave us the means to pursue major chain accounts and to acquire competitors. Because the market has become somewhat saturated, the best way for us to grow going forward is to acquire portfolios that contain a large percentage of heavily used ATMs. For example, we recently acquired a company whose portfolio contained a high percentage of major oil business, and we're going after chain store accounts whose portfolios are coming up for renewal. In terms of new accounts, the low-hanging fruit has been picked off the tree, so to speak, so we had to revise our strategy for growth.

Image Is Something

Acquiring customers was difficult in the early days, without name recognition and when there wasn't a lot of capital. We chose to target mom-and-pop businesses because we didn't have to advertise; people heard of us by word of mouth through sales calls. We remained very low-key through 1999, doing our business quietly, working hard and building a customer base. In hindsight this was a good strategy, because we didn't encounter a lot of competitive pressure. We also didn't spend money on advertising or trade shows, which at that time wouldn't have enhanced our ability to grow. We reinvested our money on expanding the company and branched out when it was beneficial to do so.

Recognition from achievement awards has helped us build image without significant cost. Also, attending important trade association shows and having the right presence at those shows is crucial. At the National Association of Convenience Stores (NACS) show this year we had an outstanding booth that enhanced our image tremendously. We have also been able to get name recognition by joining industry associations. We are on the boards of the ATM Industry Association (ATMIA) and the Electronic Funds Transfer Association (EFTA), a very prestigious group concerned with the electronic funds transfer business. EFTA protects the industry from onerous regulation and helps in the formulation of good policy. Recognition also arrived through press releases related to our business success.

With our current growth strategy, advertising is necessary and beneficial in building recognition and image, and we have joined forces with a marketing company to accomplish this.

Risks: Focus on the Core Business

Being entrepreneurial involves taking risks in the formulation and execution of a business plan. I tend to be unafraid to take a calculated risk, and I've been involved in other ventures that didn't turn out well. I learned a lot by taking those risks and losing money, and I've applied those lessons to this business.

When taking a risk, you can't be foolhardy; you have to evaluate not only the financial, but also the political and social ramifications of your decision. At Cardtronics, we manage risk by sticking to our core business and not getting too far astray, and by thorough analysis of what we do. There is plenty of growth to be had through acquisitions and contracts with large chains, and we can acquire that business by being better and more resourceful than our competitors. We evaluate decisions as a group and rely heavily on our investors for advice. I think staying focused on the core business is the key to managing risk. Getting too diversified is the wrong thing to do for a company of our size.

A Stake in the Company

Fortunately, I was entrepreneurial enough in 1996 to recognize that I had something good going on but needed help. I gave away 25 percent of the business to entice some very talented people to come in with me, which was the best thing I could have done. It is amazing how dedicated people are when they have a stake in the business. It is not uncommon for some senior employees here to work 60 or more hours a week. This is a very exciting, progressive, and profitable business, and when you get a piece of revenue from every transaction, you tend to stay motivated. The effect is almost circular: The revenue keeps growing; the profits keep growing; and your company keeps progressing because talented people have a stake in it.

I put a lot of trust in other people, and I tend to listen to input from all our managers. My employees have a lot of latitude to make their own decisions and to represent the company when visiting with customers. I try to manage by objectives and don't intervene along the way, except for progress reports. The company is small enough that the staff can convene quickly and easily to discuss *ad hoc* problems that arise.

Bonuses are used as a motivational tool. Fair compensation and a good work environment are critical to retaining and motivating people. We are well-known in the industry for our honesty, sincerity, capability, exceptional customer service, and integrity. Our good reputation inspires a lot of camaraderie among staff and continues to fuel the company's growth.

Heed Mother's Advice

The best piece of entrepreneurial advice I've ever received came from my mother, who always said, "Stick to your knitting." By that she meant stick to what you are doing: Focus on your work, and solve the problems in your way. One piece of advice I like to give is, "Don't assume." If you do, more than likely you'll be wrong. Go and seek out the facts. When the facts are there to be found, find them and use them to influence your direction.

The following is more advice I would give to entrepreneurs:

❑ Stay focused on core principles.

❑ Crawl before you walk, and walk before you run.

❑ Keep a close watch on expenses and revenue.

❑ Build your credit.

❑ Be honest and forthright with customers, vendors, and business associates.

❑ Maintain a high level of customer service.

❑ As you grow, improve your managerial talent.

❑ Do things early and on time.

❑ Plan every day as you move through the year, and formally plan at least once a year on a corporate basis.

❑ Try to always maintain an excellent reputation.

❑ Maintain high moral standards.

Looking to the Future

The financial services industry touches every member of society. Everyone has to manage money somehow. At Cardtronics we are excited because we're on the forefront of technology in financial services. Through delivery of cash, we in turn have an opportunity to provide a vital service to members of society that tangibly affects their lives. That ability is exciting because it presents a continuous stream of challenges that allow us to grow and improve our business by constantly staying on top of the latest in technology and delivering services that customers need.

For example, we're seeing a movement toward more high-tech functionality in ATMs. As the industry continues to upgrade its infrastructure using computer-based machines that run on Windows and connect to the Internet, new services will be available to consumers. Using this technology, newer ATMs that offer additional services beyond the simple cash withdrawal and balance statement – such as selling movie or theater tickets, dispensing in-store coupons, and offering access to Internet surfing – will become more widespread. The possibilities are endless, but one thing is certain: We will surely see much more and different uses of plastic cards in the near future.

It's also a very exciting time for the financial services industry as a whole because we are seeing several advancements in technology that will improve the security and services that we in the industry offer to our customers. On the security front, for example, we'll probably be seeing the use of biometric devices become more widespread and affordable. Instead of having to remember a PIN to key in, people will be able to access their money by scanning their fingerprints, palm prints, or retinas, which will make identity theft much more difficult. It will also be a convenience to the customer, because we know how difficult it is to remember PINs that you constantly have to change for security.

On the service front, there's been a great deal of discussion about the industry moving toward using "smart" cards, which use embedded computer chips to store information. Smart cards can store things like financial records, bank balances, and frequent flyer miles more securely than using the current magnetic strip technology. The idea has gained a lot of ground in Europe because they don't have existing infrastructure to replace, as we do here, but eventually these changes will come. It's conceivable that in the future everybody could be carrying around a single card for all their financial and identification needs.

Another new use for cards we're seeing recently is for initiating automated clearinghouse (ACH) transactions. While checks are not going away, using cards to distribute welfare, unemployment, and food stamp monies is much more efficient and cost-effective than mailing out paper checks each month.

Since the government is the primary source for these activities, if they could set up the infrastructure initially, that could open up a flood of possibilities for paperless financial transactions.

Changes in the industry are driven by only one thing: customer demand. In our free-market economy, if there is demand in the market for a specific product or service that makes people's lives easier, someone will fill that need. Inversely, what hurts the industry is having an outside authority mandate products and services that don't fill a commensurate market need, especially without due input from the industry.

I think history has shown us that the key to long-term success for any industry is to allow market forces to dictate the growth and business practices of individual companies, with a minimum of government interference. Self-regulation should be the first option, with outside mandate reserved as a last resort.

Industry Challenges and Customer Service

I see two main challenges in this industry. First, finances are a very sensitive issue. Customers can easily and understandably get emotional when an ATM withdrawal, credit card charge, or loan is declined. Cardtronics is successful in the financial services business because we understand people. Our customer service people are trained to deliver service in a professional way while remaining sensitive to the customer's emotional involvement with their finances.

A constantly changing technology landscape is our second major challenge. We have to deal with every change in speed, storage, and equipment technology; updating obsolete technology; and addressing how new technology improvements can be incorporated into existing systems – all with a goal of no downtime for our customers.

The golden rule of business in the financial services industry is customer service, customer service, and customer service. We must always remember that financial services are commodities. Every customer is always within reach of hundreds of sources for their financial services needs, such as ATM machines, banks, point-of-sale devices, and credit unions. If a customer receives bad service at any point, he or she may not return – there are too many alternatives available.

Our philosophy is, whatever the transaction, the customer is king. Give every customer only the best quality and service. If there's a problem, acknowledge it and correct the problem immediately. Cardtronics operates on this principle all day, every day for every customer. That's why anyone can put an ATM on the ground, but only companies that follow these guidelines can build successful businesses.

Ralph H. Clinard, president, chief executive officer, and founder, oversees the strategic direction and growth of Cardtronics. He holds a BS in mathematics from Muskingum College and a BS in mechanical engineering from Pennsylvania State University.

Mr. Clinard served with Exxon from 1957 to 1986, when he voluntarily accepted the benefits of an early retirement package offered to all professionals with required tenure. During his service, Mr. Clinard worked in a number of assignments, including products research, marketing technical services, aviation sales, advertising, business product line management, and sales management.

FINDING A WAY

JAMES C. SMITH
Webster Financial Corporation
Chairman and Chief Executive Officer

The Challenge of Growth

On a crisp, chilly October day in 1992, my father and I waited in my office, which had been his office until he retired as chief executive officer in 1987, for the up or down phone call from the Office of Thrift Supervision (OTS). Webster's COO and our CFO sat around the small, circular conference table. A tense, expectant silence was broken only occasionally by meaningless chitchat, as we had all come to believe that our future might rest on the words we would soon hear. Within two minutes of the promised 10 a.m. call, the phone rang. My heart raced as I picked up the receiver. The regulator on the other end of the phone said that the OTS in Washington had approved our bid to acquire a $1 billion failed bank in a market immediately contiguous to ours. Since only I could hear the good news, I gave a thumbs-up to the others. I could barely look at my father, as this was such an emotional moment for both of us (neither of us would admit that, of course, at the time).

It had been a long shot from the beginning – the notion of our $700 million savings and loan buying a company bigger than we were – knowing we would need bridge capital from the FDIC to meet the capital requirements. Webster's "We Find a Way" brand of today evolved from Webster's long record of finding a way to achieve our goals, in this case by knowing the failed bank acquisition rules and using them to our advantage; by having previously bought a small failed bank, while simultaneously selling off all loans to avoid any credit risk while we were in the learning process; by meeting the liquidation principal in the FDIC Washington office; and by finding a way to "run into" the chairman of the FDIC and the Resolution Liquidation chairman during their lunch hours in the cafeteria atop the FDIC building in Washington.

This was truly a stretch, but we believed in ourselves and in our ability to prevail against long odds. Nine months of intensive activity – lobbying, due diligence, even prayer – had culminated in this brief transformational phone conversation.

My father founded Webster in 1935 during the Depression to help people buy and build their homes. I joined the bank in 1975, became president in 1982, and became chief executive officer upon my father's retirement from that position in 1987. We had converted from a mutual to a publicly traded company at the end of 1986. Our strategic plan called for growth through geographic expansion and broadening and deepening of our product lines with the goal of making a transition to a commercial bank-like financial services provider.

There weren't many banks to buy in the heady commercial real estate boom in the late 1980s, but the inevitable and protracted downturn in the early 1990s created enormous opportunity for our institution. We had built capital and management capability in the interim and had shied away from high-risk commercial real estate lending. Asset quality was always a strength at Webster. We could underwrite with the best of them, and when the risk of a transaction or a market trend seemed greater than the potential reward, we hunkered down.

We were and are today guided by my father's three-pronged rule. One, always remember you are in the business of taking risk (credit risk, interest rate risk, transaction risk, capital risk, or reputation risk). Two, never take a risk you cannot afford. And three, make sure you know the difference between one and two. The wisdom of the rule had started to sink in by the time my father and I went up in what my son calls the "bucket loader" in 1995 to change the sign at our headquarters location to Webster Bank in honor of my father, whose name was Harold Webster Smith. He died in 1997, still chairman emeritus of the company he founded 62 years before.

It was only years later that I could fully appreciate how much confidence my father had in me and in our team to support us unequivocally in the months leading to that defining moment in 1991. We put all of the institution's capital on the line, and then some, thanks to the FDIC bridge loan, on the expectation that we could manage the myriad risks associated with acquiring a failed institution in a transaction that more than doubled our size. We reminisce today about how we became a $2 billion bank on the same day we became a $1 billion bank. Of course, today we're thinking about becoming a $20 billion, or $30 billion bank. Some things never change – like that constant Webster desire to grow and to improve.

It wasn't long until acquisition and integration of like-minded Connecticut banks became a core strength at Webster. One out of every four independent Connecticut banks in 1991 is part of Webster today. We have expanded our acquisition expertise to include insurance agencies (we bought five) and trust companies (we bought two). We bought a leasing company and an asset-based lender. We bought a financial valuation and advisory firm. Webster is a growth company, dedicated to building strong customer relationships that increase shareholder value, focused on internal growth and external acquisitions, in relentless pursuit of value creation.

In the course of the past decade Webster Financial Corporation has grown from that small thrift I described to become the largest Connecticut-based bank, as measured by assets, market capitalization, and profitability. Webster today provides a broad range of financial services for the purpose of helping individuals, families, and businesses achieve their financial goals – a mission not dissimilar from the one mandated by our initial federal charter, which was to "provide a safe and convenient method for people to save and invest while promoting the sound and economical financing of homes."

The Sources of Growth

Our growth comes from several sources. The deregulation of the banking and financial services industry, advances in technology, a focus on strategy, and skillful execution are all part of the mix.

Consistent with our "taking risks" philosophy, we try to understand and mitigate risk so as to balance the risk/reward equation in our favor. Sure, we take risk by growing rapidly, but we mitigate those risks by recruiting people with specialized knowledge and experience whom we trust to execute our plan. By expanding into different businesses, we spread the risk and strengthen the earnings stream simultaneously. We thrive on taking calculated risks as we evolve our business model.

We try to take "bite-size risks." For example, we may buy an insurance agency, but not one so big that it will have a negative impact on our capitalization. We can then attract talent and build from there – we learn as we go. This appreciation for assumption of appropriate risks is Webster's greatest strength. This is also how we got into the commercial banking business. We have thrived on understanding and appreciating risk, knowing how precious our capital is, and investing it carefully, while advancing our strategic plan.

Risk has traditionally been associated with taking action. Given the pace of consolidation and convergence in the financial services industry today, there is also risk – survival risk – in being too cautious. One of Darwin's most important lessons was that survival is not a function of speed or strength or endurance – it is a function of adaptability. Webster has sought to avoid danger, but at the same time, we have aggressively sought to adapt to the opportunities suddenly offered by the changing financial services industry.

We believe that change agents are by definition risk takers. Our commitments to growth and change have had notably positive results. During the past five years our total assets have increased from $4 billion to $12 billion; our operating earnings from $29 million to $138 million; and our market capital from $291 million to $1.8 billion. Our earnings per share have grown faster than those of our peers, and so has our total shareholder return.

I expect and hope that the need to adapt and to lead change in this highly competitive world will continue at a demanding pace. Rapid change means you have to be on top of your game all the time. You must be able to improve yourself continuously and adapt to the changing environment to be successful. That sense of urgency must be felt throughout the organization.

The most exciting part of my job is the constant change that our industry is undergoing, and the opportunity this provides for us to grow and expand our capabilities in an environment where there is continual consolidation and convergence. Webster is carving out its place as a provider of financial services on a much broader platform than we could have imagined 10 years ago. It's exciting because with significant change comes boundless opportunity and the thrill of performing well in a highly competitive market.

For more than a decade there has been an inexorable consolidation in the banking industry that more recently is giving way to a convergence among banks, insurance companies, securities brokers, and investment bankers. We look at the Citigroup of today and admire the remarkably broad capabilities it can provide for its customers. In one corner we have this highly capitalized global competitor with one-stop shopping capabilities serving a spectrum from small consumers to huge corporations. At the other end of the spectrum are small community banks providing highly personalized services to local consumers and small businesses.

We're in the middle, which is right where we want to be: sufficient capital, a regional franchise, and a breadth of financial services with significant local knowledge and a strong connection to all of our communities. More of our customers can take more of their services from us, and we've learned how to make sure they have the opportunity to do so. With consolidation and convergence come benefit and opportunity. Customers enjoy our greater financial strength, broader choice, and heightened convenience from our extensive branch network, ATMs, call center and Internet services. On the other hand, smaller organizations that truly understand their markets can thrive, based on the strength of the customer relationships they build. Customers today can choose along a spectrum from big, strong, and diversified all the way to smaller, local, and very personal.

Role of the Board of Directors

Webster has been blessed with a forward-thinking, fully engaged board of directors that has encouraged and authorized our growth and expansion plans over the past decade. Through its Corporate Governance Committee, the board ensures that its makeup evolves in tandem with the growth and complexity of the institution.

As companies grow, the qualifications and skills of the ideal board change. Webster's board has implemented director qualifications that reinforce the board's commitment to provide relevant leadership as the institution grows and changes. In particular, the board's participation in the strategic planning process has contributed to a cycle of confidence between the officers and directors and has raised our overall confidence in our ability to achieve our ambitious goals.

Keys to Success

When we renamed Webster in honor of my father in 1995, we also adopted a value system that our employees believe captured the essence of Webster. In effect, we institutionalized the principles that had guided the institution for decades. As we grew rapidly, we wanted our employees to know what Webster stands for. They could appreciate the elements that represented Webster's strong foundation – its unshakable core – which creates unlimited opportunity for the people who are Webster to grow personally and professionally as they contribute to Webster's growth and progress.

The "Webster Way," which many of our employees can cite by heart, and which all of our employees see day-in and day-out, is simple and straightforward, and it's ours. Its application goes well beyond the job and for many represents a way of life:

❑ We take personal responsibility for meeting our customers' financial needs.

❑ We respect the dignity of every individual.

❑ We earn people's confidence through ethical behavior.

❑ We give of ourselves in the communities we serve.

❑ We strive for excellence in everything we do.

To me, the Webster Way is the context in which we compete aggressively, yet respectfully; passionately, yet considerately.

Knowing that our employees are bound together by the Webster Way, we can communicate confidently with our market in a style that will convey over and over again what we stand for. Our highly focused, customer-oriented attitude is one of the keys to our success; we will go the extra mile to make certain we serve our customers well. This concept resonates internally, leveraging our values. Our employees are our most vital resource. I believe they are unusual in their ability to make such a good impression on our customers and then follow through with results.

Every one of our employees who have direct contact with customers receives special training and development guidance, so that he or she can appreciate how each situation appears from the customer's perspective. First, we try to be pleasant and attentive, provide good service, staff our offices appropriately, and meet many other criteria of good customer service. We also have what we call a consultative selling approach, wherein our employees are trained to know what questions to ask a customer to help them make the best choices for their financial future. We try to develop our employees' knowledge of all our products and services, but we can always call in product-area specialists to help assist customers who have specific product needs. Ultimately, our relationship with our customers will determine our relationship in the market overall. We put providing good, solid customer service at the top of our list, and we invest heavily to make that happen.

Technology is the single most critical factor driving growth in financial services companies today. The ability to process, store, access, manage, and report information has created clear competitive advantage for larger institutions. It is a fact that greater technological capacity spread over a growing customer base produces lower unit processing costs. At long last, bigger can truly mean more efficient. It also makes it harder to be really small and be competitive on the unit cost side.

I would not say that we are a technology leader, but we appreciate technology's value to our business plan. We process, store, and retrieve information more efficiently than ever before. While we may not be as technologically advanced as some of our larger competitors, we are far enough up the curve to be competitive. In some areas, including our Web site, unfettered by huge legacy systems, we are near the lead in innovation.

Today we have nearly $5 million in assets per Webster employee, about two-thirds higher than our asset-to-employee ratio a decade ago. Where we might have needed three employees to handle a certain amount of business before, two employees can handle it today. The beauty of this progress to Webster is that it occurs in a growth company – we employ 2,500 people today versus 200 ten years ago – so our existing employees have the opportunity to take on more responsibility due to technology gains. They don't have to fear for their livelihood every time we enhance our systems' capabilities.

A balanced revenue model is another key to success, and we've made remarkable progress in this regard. Today 30 percent of our revenue comes from fee-based services, up from 10 percent about five years ago. We expect that number will rise to 40 percent over the next three years. Half of our fee-based revenue is from businesses we had not entered five years ago. The beauty of these fee-based businesses, particularly investment management and our insurance agency, is that they require minimal capital and will contribute to a reliable, growing, recurring earnings stream, which in turn will increase the value of our earnings and, we hope, boost our price/earnings ratio.

One positive effect of the economic turbulence of 2002 is that interest rates are lower, especially over the near term. In terms of revenue generation, this has been a positive that has offset the negatives that come from slower loan growth and the inevitably higher level of non-performing assets that a bank will experience in a weaker economy. As the economy strengthens, short rates will raise. This might have a negative impact on spread income, but should be offset by higher loan volume and higher fee-based revenue. Our revenue model therefore can be pretty reliable, despite the challenges of the economic environment in which we are operating.

For us, the glass is always half-full, regardless of the economic situation. If a turbulent environment makes it harder for some institutions to grow, it will make them more likely to take a responsible partner – like Webster. Since our well-developed growth plans protect us in good markets and bad and will help us continue to grow faster than our smaller brethren, we have become an attractive partner for those who choose to join forces. We can either grow naturally in good environments or through taking partners in weaker environments.

Relying on Employee Expertise

We recognize that the people who run our business units are the experts, and that they must be enabled to make decisions they need to make to advance their business lines. In the old days we could make most of the decisions with a small group of executives. In fact, in the old, old days, my father was able to make many of the strategic decisions himself. He and I both recognized that the primary organizational shift would be a transition from an autocratic style to an organization that values and needs expertise in each of its lines of business and in all of the support areas, as well.

Today Webster has evolved to a point where I spend most of my time on the planning, recruitment, and corporate development side. I make sure the strategic plan is linked to the financial plans and that the financial plans are aligned with the incentive plans, and then encourage and rely on our highly capable group of officers and employees to execute those plans successfully. The ultimate objective, of course, is value creation – in our case attained by building strong customer relationships that increase shareholder value and driven by broadening and deepening existing relationships and increasing market share and through sound, value-adding acquisitions.

Regarding Webster's management capabilities, the consolidation in the industry has benefited us because there are many high-quality people in the market who might not otherwise have been available to us. We have been fortunate to be able to attract more than our share of these high-quality people. They include capable executives who have decided to opt out of the mega-company life in favor of becoming a more meaningful part of a smaller, growing company.

Also, our rapid growth has brought us to a size at which we can better afford to attract higher-end talent to manage our growing businesses. I think we have also benefited from having a good reputation in the market. We've been a responsible acquisition partner. We've performed relatively well. We have clear momentum as we strive to become a regional competitive force. These characteristics have helped us attract high-caliber, motivated employees to Webster. It has been a bit of good fortune that as we have developed our business plan in a rapidly consolidating market, we've been able to attract these talented people, while at the same time developing people from within to achieve our goals.

When we look for new executives, we expect them to know their businesses well, make good decisions, and appreciate the opportunities for growth. They must be able to build a strategic plan that has a high-growth component, and they must work under the rule of capital allocation and bear the cost of the capital that is allocated to their businesses. We look for ambitious, intelligent, highly motivated people who want to be part of a team that is moving smartly forward and believes in itself.

A lot of mutual trust is involved in the relationship between Webster and its employees. Trustworthiness is an absolute requirement for every member of the team. My father used to remind me that any strong relationship is built on trust. To boil it down even further – he was a master of distilling matters to their essence – he said, "Trust begins and ends with truth." Officers operating within a set of guidelines take most of the risks we take today at Webster. Guided, protected, and when necessary, limited by strong and closely monitored internal controls, these leaders generally take the right risks and make the right decisions on Webster's behalf. We trust them to operate within the parameters upon which we have mutually agreed.

Most of our employees have their success measured against a clear-cut set of agreed-upon goals they are expected to achieve in a particular year. If they achieve these quantitative and qualitative goals, they receive awards at a target level agreed to in advance. If they exceed their goals, they receive a higher award. Likewise, if they fall short of their goals, they receive less reward. Our compensation programs are built in such a way that outstanding performance is rewarded with outstanding compensation.

There is always an opportunity for people to earn above-average compensation based on their performance. They are also able to participate in our long-term incentive plans, whereby they will benefit directly as the value of our currency rises, which is directly related to the impact of their contributions. Our long-term investment plans have helped align the interest of every Webster employee to Webster's strategic plan.

Leadership, Teamwork and Motivation

We believe in the inherent capacity of every individual, and especially Webster employees, to exceed expectations, and we try to develop them and motivate them accordingly.

Hugely important in a fast-growing organization is continual reassessment of its senior people. One of the risks we cannot afford is to grow beyond our capabilities as a management team. We are ever-sensitive to this possibility and are constantly reassessing our capabilities and renewing ourselves, not only to manage the financial services company we have become, but with an eye toward always doubling in size and complexity. To date, because of the talent in the market and the capabilities of longer-term Webster employees, we have assembled a remarkably strong mix of talent that will propel us to the next level and beyond. The Webster value system has also been vitally important in maintaining the unshakable core on which our management principles are built.

Having a good team, properly motivated and focused on growth and productivity, are necessary conditions for success. Good communication is another must in a healthy, growing organization. Employees who are out front, meeting with customers and executing programs, know what is going on and need to share that vital, current information. People with key leadership roles listen carefully to be sure they are up to speed and have the benefit of news from the marketplace. Managers communicate directly with their respective teams. While we use e-mail, corporatewide instant messaging, and other new forms of conveying information, the best way to communicate remains face-to-face meetings, discussions, and interchange between supervisor and the team he or she leads. That's the best way to be sure of agreement on priorities and to have mutual understanding. At Webster we try to "cascade" news quickly and thoroughly from managers to their teams through direct, human communication.

To help motivate employees, I try to get out in the field, hold town hall meetings, send e-mails out to our employees, and meet regularly with the senior group. We work hard to make certain there is good communication overall, so our employees understand our corporate direction. They appreciate communication and try to achieve our overall goals, as well as the goals within their particular business units. I think the best way to have people appreciate what we are all about is just to be "real," honest, and straightforward and to remember our responsibility to the people who work here. After that, it is pretty simple.

Another important point is that we believe that every employee, regardless of title or duties, has a personal responsibility to earn and receive the respect of those around him or her every day. We are all of us peers in that we are individuals performing at the highest level in the positions we occupy in the organization. Our culture is intended to promote connectivity and collaboration.

Our "We Find a Way" attitude and our Webster Way values are not intended to build a cult-like environment, but rather to engender a sense of community that can extend beyond the company to the way we live our lives. We celebrate individual achievement in a team context. We reward teamwork as a qualitative measurement. We believe in clear ownership for generating the best results, with those results achieved for the greater benefit of the whole and not at the expense of the broader enterprise.

My father was right, as usual, when he told me 20 years ago upon my being named president, that my responsibilities would be significantly different from his. He said he had spent most of his time executing a clear-cut, highly focused plan, determined in large part by tight regulatory boundaries. My career would be spent managing organizational development, building and implementing longer-range strategies, and communicating clearly and effectively to a highly skilled and diverse workforce. My success would ultimately be determined by the wisdom of the plan and how well we followed it, by the skills and quality of the people on the team and how they were organized, and by the strength of the message and the manner in which it was communicated.

As we manage our larger organizations with bigger ambitions still, we've learned that to operate effectively in our fast-paced, fast-changing environment, structure is essential. Growth requires structural change. Organization and structure are required if change is to be effectively communicated and achieved in a larger company. Talent assessment, leadership development, personal development plans, and ongoing training become key to human resources management efforts. Technology must be understood and appreciated as a tool for productivity and communication. Recognizing the requirements of managing successfully in a larger organization is the first step toward gaining buy-in and sincere commitment to investing in our human resources.

The most important thing I've learned as a manager over the years is that in a larger organization, if you want to make something happen, you must have the organized capacity to achieve your goal. You must have mechanisms in place to track progress against plans that measure results. Those mechanisms are the means by which people are constantly reminded of their commitment to produce, to succeed, to change. The mechanisms are necessary, whether we are talking about implementing a strategy, linking a financial plan to an incentive plan, or perpetuating a true value system. Ideas dissipate unless they can take life in the form of a plan with commitments made, resources allocated, and measurements agreed upon. Our commitment to regular, repetitive, relentless, recurring communication and training – where important plans and principles are involved – is serving us well.

If you are reading this chapter five years after I have written it and you click onto the Webster Web site to check on our progress (and we hope you'll open a relationship with Webster while you're there!), you'll find a strong, independent regional financial services provider to which the phrase "more and better" will apply well. Our franchise will have grown through contiguous expansion, greater penetration of the market, deeper customer relationships, and acquisitions of like-minded institutions. We'll be at least twice our current size. We'll be listed among the top 50 banks in America.

In all of our primary businesses – consumer, mortgage, and commercial banking, insurance services, trust and investment management, financial advisory services, and equipment leasing and financing – 80 percent of our customer transactions will occur through automated means, with unit processing costs significantly lower than today. Our revenues will exceed

$1 billion, double today's revenue, of which 40 percent or more will be from fee-based services.

We will continue to enjoy the confidence of our shareholders by meeting or exceeding expectations and by our successful efforts to build and sustain a growing, reliable, recurring earnings stream. The Webster community will be bigger and stronger, sustained by the all-important unshakable core. We will still be doing what we do best – finding a way to help our customers achieve their financial goals. We will have taken risks, but none that we could not afford. Perhaps our very good company, as it continues to exceed expectations, will by then be seen as one of America's great companies.

James C. Smith is chairman and CEO of Webster Financial Corporation. He joined the company in 1975 and has served as chief executive officer since 1987. Under his direction Webster Bank has developed and executed a strategic plan to become the largest Connecticut-based bank, while Webster Insurance is the largest Connecticut-based insurance agency.

Mr. Smith is cochair, with Connecticut Governor John Rowland, of the Governor's Council on Economic Competitiveness and Technology. His board memberships include corporate, trade association, and charitable organization service. He was the 2001 chairman of the United Way of the Capital Area Community Campaign. Mr. Smith is a graduate of Dartmouth College.

BEST SELLING BOOKS

REFERENCE

Business Travel Bible – Must Have Phone Numbers, Business Resources & Maps
The Golf Course Locator for Business Professionals – Golf Courses Closest to Largest Companies, Law Firms, Cities & Airports
Business Grammar, Style & Usage – Rules for Articulate and Polished Business Writing and Speaking
ExecRecs – Executive Recommendations For The Best Business Products & Services
Living Longer Working Stronger – Simple Steps for Business Professionals to Capitalize on Better Health
The C-Level Test – Business IQ & Personality Test for Professionals of All Levels
The Business Translator-Business Words, Phrases & Customs in Over 65 Languages
Small Business Bible – Phone Numbers, Business Resources, Financial, Tax & Legal Info
The Small Business Checkup – A Planning & Brainstorming Workbook for Your Business

MANAGEMENT

Corporate Ethics – The Business Code of Conduct for Ethical Employees
The Governance Game – Restoring Boardroom Excellence & Credibility in America
Inside the Minds: Leading CEOs – CEOs Reveal the Secrets to Leadership & Profiting in Any Economy
Inside the Minds: The Entrepreneurial Problem Solver – Entrepreneurial Strategies for Identifying Opportunities in the Marketplace
Inside the Minds: Leading Consultants – Industry Leaders Share Their Knowledge on the Art of Consulting
Being There Without Going There: Managing Teams Across Time Zones, Locations and Corporate Boundaries

TECHNOLOGY

Inside the Minds: Leading CTOs – The Secrets to the Art, Science & Future of Technology
Software Product Management – Managing Software Development from Idea to Development to Marketing to Sales
Inside the Minds: The Telecommunications Industry – Leading CEOs Share Their Knowledge on The Future of the Telecommunications Industry
Web 2.0 AC (After Crash) – The Resurgence of the Internet and Technology Economy
Inside the Minds: The Semiconductor Industry – Leading CEOs Share Their Knowledge on the Future of Semiconductors

VENTURE CAPITAL/ENTREPRENEURIAL

Term Sheets & Valuations – A Detailed Look at the Intricacies of Term Sheets & Valuations

Deal Terms – The Finer Points of Deal Structures, Valuations, Term Sheets, Stock Options and Getting Deals Done

Inside the Minds: The Ways of the VC – Identifying Opportunities, Assessing Business Models and What it Takes to Land an Investment From a VC

Inside the Minds: Leading Deal Makers – Leveraging Your Position and the Art of Deal Making

Inside the Minds: Entrepreneurial Momentum – Gaining Traction for Businesses of All Sizes to Take the Step to the Next Level

Inside the Minds: The Entrepreneurial Problem Solver – Entrepreneurial Strategies for Identifying Opportunities in the Marketplace

Inside the Minds: JumpStart – Launching Your Business Venture, Profitably and Successfully

FINANCIAL

Inside the Minds: Leading Accountants – The Golden Rules of Accounting & the Future of the Accounting Industry and Profession

Inside the Minds: Leading Investment Bankers – Leading I-Bankers Reveal the Secrets to the Art & Science of Investment Banking

Inside the Minds: The Financial Services Industry – The Future of the Financial Services Industry & Professions

Building a $1,000,000 Nest Egg – 10 Strategies to Gaining Wealth at Any Age

Inside the Minds: The Return of Bullish Investing

Inside the Minds: The Invincibility Shield for Investors

MARKETING/ADVERTISING/PR

Inside the Minds: Leading Marketers–Leading Chief Marketing Officers Reveal the Secrets to Building a Billion Dollar Brand

Inside the Minds: Leading Advertisers – Advertising CEOs Reveal the Tricks of the Advertising Profession

Inside the Minds: The Art of PR – Leading PR CEOs Reveal the Secrets to the Public Relations Profession

Inside the Minds: PR Visionaries – PR CEOS Reveal the Golden Rules to Becoming a Senior Partner With Your Clients

Inside the Minds: The Art of Building a Brand – Leading Advertising & PR CEOs Reveal the Secrets Behind Successful Branding Strategies

The Best of Guerrilla Marketing – Marketing on a Shoestring Budget